Hang on.

Help is on its way.

On my front porch near the berry bush. Summer 1977
Northeastern USA

help is on its way

a true story

‡‡

jenna forrest

A BookSurge Publication

Copyright © 2008 by Jenna Forrest

Cover Design by Mimosa Mallernee
Edited by Molly McKitterick

Lyrics Permission Licensed by Alfred Publishing Co. Inc.

ISBN-13: 978-0-9792298-1-7
ISBN-10: 0-9792298-1-2

Manufactured in the United States of America
Third Edition: February 2008

For more information, please visit www.jennaforrest.com

Dedication

This memoir is dedicated to those who experience life through highly tuned senses; physical senses like keen sight, hearing, touch, taste and smell, or perhaps a developed "sixth sense" evidenced by broad empathy, creative inspiration, vivid dreaming, extrasensory perception, complex imagination, and divine intervention.

Thank you for being the deep and perceptive ones among us and for being consciencious workers, thoughtful partners and insightful leaders. Thank you for your intellectual and creative contributions to the world, for your passionate focus and compassionate hearts. May your innate gifts be valued, validated and nurtured in the world and within your own souls.

Acknowledgements

To the steadfast faith, encouragement, kindness and
generosity of the people I am honored to have in my life.

With gratefulness to my God, my guide.

Prologue

None like this
Birth, 1971

I want to reverse time back before Mom was pregnant and freeze it there so my spirit can just keep flying free in the unseen space between universes. I have this dream of spirit that disconnects me from Earth's grainy human reality, facts and matter. My bubbling urge is to return to celestial switchbacks in the sky without the weight of a body. I won't be dead, no. Remained unborn, yes.

Having been given life, I feel defeated, sour and rejected. It's because I've been displaced by an afterworld that wanted me here on Earth despite my beseeching to stay there. The world is already forming gnarls around me, knots that spring vines aimed at me joining the human race. It makes me deeply melancholy.

I'll soon forget why I'm so sad. The instructive voice of the divine will have faded against the busy hiss of this planet I am both occupying and resisting. From this moment on, society will continue to grow louder, its undertow stronger, doling out circumstances that will force me into the unpleasant tasks of interacting, participating and contributing like a so-called person.

With such involvement will come a personal investment in the world's unfair conditions. I will be surrounded by souls who are suffering and I will be one of them. My only hope will be the pivotal reversal of my own desperation. I will remember to talk to a realm beyond this one, asking for help to come. And that will be the beginning of my way back, recalling my origination and getting clear on my purpose on this planet.

Now one last important point before I begin forgetting...

Having lived this history, I will have no regrets. It will have been nothing but a story's unearthing, for any other situation would have left this book unwritten.

1

Drawings of My Street
Age 6, 1977

There's a smell of apples in the air. The candied kind, with nuts stuck to them. It's coming from the carnival at Holy Family, the Catholic school at the end of my street. This spot on my front steps earns me a good view of the parade of people leaving the festival. Families and friends are marching in tight clusters with armfuls of leftover cotton candy, popcorn, stuffed animals and bags of goldfish.

I naturally assume their liveliness and excitement as they pass by me. The buzz of their joyfulness makes me dream a wish. I want those people to all go home and do great things for the world. Because the world needs those kinds of people; hearty people who do great things, big things with their hearts, for the world.

I work best on my drawings here on the cracked concrete steps because being here near the old tree trunks and under their leafy limbs makes me feel protected from the heavy hand of the world. This sacred spot is my only safe container.

It would be nice to draw a picture that would show my parents what goes on inside my head so they would stop asking what's wrong with me—why I'm so deep, so careful. But it would take mountains of paper and rivers of paint to draw that picture. So instead I'll draw simple pictures on letter-sized paper, like the ones my older sister

Toni makes, with princesses and fashions and trees with red apples.

Quiet times like this give me a break from having to feel everyone else's feelings. It's better to feel my own. When I do, a strong knowing comes inside me that I have big things to do with my heart for the world, too. The idea of it makes me shiver and beam. I rake the stair step below me with my fingers to clasp an orange heart shaped leaf, which I know is a clue telling me yes, keep believing in such good things; you're on the right track.

There's this bush right beside my spot here on the steps that looks just like the apple trees my sister draws. It's round and green and seems lit up with bright red berries.

Mom must have known I wanted to eat those berries the first day we moved here since she made a point to tell me and Toni not to eat them. She instructed us very clearly saying "Be sure to leave those berries alone. They're poisonous to people. They're only good for birds." And of course that very second I wanted to be a bird so I could fly down and eat the bright berries right off of the bush.

Dropping my paper and crayons, I take a good look at what makes for a poison berry. It's just good manners to take a closer peek at the things nature has put out there for you to see. *Snap, snap, snap*, the berries drop off easy, like they almost wanted to be plucked. The peanut sized fruits look so bright and juicy in my hand, like three tiny red balloons without strings, just calling to be popped.

I toss two of them aside, their weighty round juiciness bouncing once in the grass then landing for good, full and still. The third gets squished between my fingers with excited anticipation of what human poison actually looks like. A filmy blob with clear juice and tiny seeds spurts out the berry's small opening. It's not black or ugly like you'd expect poison to be, but see-through and maybe even clean, pure, like the birds who eat it.

The second I lick the mash of poison and seeds off my fingers a cramp forms tight around my stomach. Wondering about the effects of this personal experiment, I peer suspiciously toward the bush. It crosses my mind that the beauty of the berries could have been a trick to attract kids like me who are dumb enough to take chances with poison. I can't be too sure. But then again nature wouldn't do anything to hurt me. It couldn't.

I'm probably just getting that regular stomach ache that Dad says I get when I worry too much. He says I worry about everything–calls me an emotional yo-yo. I just wonder who's holding the string.

"C'mon Jenna, pick yourself up by your bootstraps," Dad said last time I was curled up with a stomach ache.

"You can't pick up your own self," I murmured. "Only other people can pick you up."

But my Dad didn't get the hint.

"Jen-naaaaa."

I shrink when Mom calls from inside the house. Sensing she's heard every thought I've been thinking all this time I don't want to answer her. I won't be able to explain why the poison was a temptation. I grasp my drawings nervously, fearing they might blow off into a trail that will lead me to be found.

I jam my hand deep into the massive berry bush beside me, fishing for a strong branch to grab and pull my body deep inside it. After a short spell of flying branches,

13

breaking twigs and shedding leaves, I rest inside my shelter, a capsule of green shrubbery.

"Jenna, come on out of there."

My Mom is a twenty seven year old square faced blonde, her small frame still tan from the summer. She's always pretty no matter what the sun does or doesn't do to her.

"What's going on?" Mom gets right to the point, never wasting a word.

She yanks up her pants at the knees to squat down to find my eyes. There's no way she can deal with my troubles. As a social worker, she fixes people's problems at work all week as it is. It's not easy finding jobs for people with disabilities, she says. So I want to give her a break when she's home.

I hug my legs tight, hoping she doesn't see me peering out at her from inside my leafy shield of armor. I'm scared that whatever she'll ask me will remind me I'm over-emotional, in other words, not normal. The worry I cause my family with my overdone emotions complicates what I'm going through. There's no justification, just more damp patches of sadness on each faded knee of my jeans.

"It looks like your senses are working overtime again, Jenna. What could you possibly be all that miserable about?"

Her eyes are alive with a crystal blue tint that makes her appear innocent and harmless, just like the berry poison. When I don't answer, she picks up one of my drawings and sees I was coloring the beginnings of a tree.

"Let's get you out of there."

Mom shoves her teased and sprayed hairdo straight towards me, way deep into the bush's bulk. If Mom is risking her hairdo, I know she's serious about reaching me. But it seems like every time she really reaches me, she lets go again much too soon. To protect myself from being abandoned by her touch I dig deeper into the center of the shrub, farther out of her grasp.

Mom's hair gets stuck on one of the limbs, making her have to back out and pinch leaves, twigs and berries from her matted head. Still, she's determined to dive in again. Holding her breath as if she's plunging under water, she extends her arms through the branches far enough to give a light encouraging tug to my elbow.

Her touch leaves a cool scent of lemon on my sleeves, giving me that feeling like I've been loaned back some part of me that's been missing. A great surge of love tempts me to leap into her arms and hold steady in a spot right close to her heart. I want her to say "I've got you" while I cry rivers for the relief of actually belonging somewhere in the world.

The neighbor's keys jingle outside their door, making Mom spring away from the bush, quickly dusting herself off.

"She's just stopped sucking her thumb and now she's hiding in a bush. Kids!" she announces to our neighbor, red-faced. And even though I'm hidden deep inside this great big bush, I still feel the need to disappear.

The neighbor knows that six years is too long to suck your thumb. Mom says it messes up your teeth and makes you swallow funny. Dad tried to get me to stop the habit by wrapping my thumb with black electrical tape at

15

night. What made me finally stop was my dentist, who said, "If you keep sucking your thumb, you'll have to take swallowing lessons."

The picture of a man who smells like a cough drop telling me what to do with my own tongue and spit made me lose the taste for my thumb completely. Now it's on to bigger problems, like figuring out once and for all what's wrong with me.

My body slumps with relief when Mom withdraws back into the house, the screen door snapping shut tight behind her. I don't even know why I want to cry again except that so much of what happens in my life makes me feel off-center. I'm forever losing at this thing called living.

I stretch out from under the bush, dust myself off, and slide back into my preferred spot at the top porch step. It's where the tree branches hang over me, sheltering me from the sky that's falling inside my head. I know one thing for sure. Trees don't need any explanations. They let you feel any way you please and just sit there with you in peace. I think that's why trees are here on earth–to give every person the chance to experience the feeling of quiet kindness at least once in their life.

It helps to sit still in nature and think about what I'm going to do about life; knowing I can't go on giving everything I have just to make it through each day.

Scribbling up my paper with crayons I finish my picture of the bright yellow oak trees on my street. In the picture the trees are emptying their branches. Their leaves have covered up all of the roads that might lead to confusing places. And there's a special golden road that I pretend will take me to a nice place that always feels safe and good to me.

I guess the carnival is over for the day because the sidewalk below my house has already cleared of people.

Setting my box of crayons on top of my drawing will keep it from blowing away while I walk down eleven concrete steps to the sidewalk. I like looking up at the leaves spinning off the granddaddy oak tree in the silent sweet air. They take their time circling above me, floating in and out of the rays of sunshine that poke through the tree branches.

It makes me remember the feeling I had last fall, daydreaming into the swirl of woodsy smells that could only mean the end of summer. It was an easy escape from my heavy feelings. I'm feeling the same peace right now, watching the sun paint bright colors over the fading green leaves. It's so pretty here. I can't help but expect that this new season will bring good things with it.

Mom says the seasons come and go in cycles. On cloudy days, she says, "Oh well, the sunshine will come find us."

I suppose the sunshine will come find me.

I just wonder how long I'll have to wait.

Christmas Day 1978
Me, left, with my sister on our front porch.

2

Tidal Wave
Age 7, 1978

Glossy album covers, record sleeves, and black vinyl discs carpet the bare wood floor around the stereo, our only piece of furniture that never gathers dust. Here on the floor by the big block speakers I can hear the words inside the music.

Lyrics will tell you a story if you let them. You can disappear all the way into a song's lyrics to feel exactly what the singer felt when writing the song. But sometimes that's dangerous. Songs about losing someone you love, saying goodbye, or feeling alone warrant bed rest from sheer sadness. Switching to cheerful songs turns the blues away, making me dance in my socks and laugh with my mouth wide open until it hurts. I take personal comfort knowing there are musicians out there who understand the good and bad of how I feel.

My parents choose to play so many songs because they need the music to feel their feelings for them. Neither of them believe in actually having feelings themselves. They say that "smart thinking makes good people," and drop big hints that crying is a waste of time. Still, you get an idea that they have more feelings than they let on because anyone who has so many whopping fights has got to be feeling something.

Mom's lacy top and slim fitting jeans make her look especially pretty today. My Mom always dresses for her figure and smells sweet with perfume. She wears a thin gold chain necklace on her collarbone making it clear to the world, especially to my Dad, that she's a woman.

Being a woman means spending entire Saturdays in the ladies section of department stores. Mom gets her makeover done at that cosmetics counter with the mirror that rotates into a magnified view. It's there to show you that no matter how good you think you look, your complexion is a nightmare that needs serious fixing. A pretty lady paints up Mom's face with a pile of assorted beauty products to demonstrate how perfect she can look this season with the right makeup. Once Mom has her face freshly blushed, shadowed and glossed the lady always forgets to show Mom her magnified face again. So last time I reminded her to look again, flipping the mirror for her.

"Still not too good," my Mom said, squinting and poking at her larger-than-life reflection.

Dad is Mom's mirror opposite. He's five hair shades darker and a whole foot taller than Mom. When you see my parents standing side by side you might think it's an effort for them to see each other because of the height distance between their eyes. But when Dad bends way down to kiss Mom, you realize they want to make the effort.

It's no sweat for my Dad to erase the distance between him and his daughters either. As big as we've gotten, he's still strong enough to scoop us both up, one in each arm, pulling our feet off the floor like we have wings. Sisters in flight. It's a whole different view from all the way up in Dad's arms. It's where my bare feet safely dangle above the serious ground that I know wants to swallow me whole.

I've heard people out in public point to Dad and say "I'd hate to mess with that guy" because from the back he looks like he could be tough and mean. But if they'd seen his face they'd have said, "I'd love to know that guy" because Dad has bright cheery eyes and wears a thick mustache capped smile wherever he goes.

He sees a joke in everything. He even makes jokes out of my serious questions to make me laugh and forget what I was asking him. It's not till later on that I realize Dad never did give me an answer. And if I had to choose between what's funny and what's true, I'd pick true a hundred times out of a hundred. That's why it's essential to look straight into my Dad's eyes now. If I look real close, I can conclude what his true answer would have been if he'd actually said it.

I'm on my belly on the floor by the speaker listening to the crackly rotation of the turntable. The pause between songs gives room to overhear Mom challenging Dad in the kitchen.

"You never take your turn taking care of the kids."

This is usually how it starts. I tell myself to keep my focus on the next James Taylor song that's just started playing on the stereo. His voice is friendly. It makes me remember that there are still gentle people in the world even if those people aren't in our house right this very instant.

"Well you're always yelling at them." Dad opens the fridge and pulls out a bottle of beer. *Clink*.

"At least I'm here for them. All you do is go out drinking with your friends!" Mom slams the refrigerator door, making the floor vibrate right where I sit in the living room.

My sister Toni and I get nervous when my parents start arguing. Toni is my only sibling, just over a year older than me. We're almost the same age and look like twins except her nose is freckled and her curly strands of hair make my wavy ones look straight. Toni is loud, loves crowds, and easily makes friends–pretty much all the things that make me want to pass out. Keeping close to her shields me.

Right now Toni's where she loves to be, in the chair across the room from me pretending to be reading. When Dad hollers, she looks up from her book with enormous blue eyes so much like Mom's.

"At least I have friends. And anyway, the kids don't need anything. Look at them. They're doing just fine."

Anybody in their right mind would flinch when Mom revolts against Dad. Even my sister puts her book down. We both sit up in attention like we might be needed for something.

"You're so lazy and self-centered. You don't care about your kids. You seem to think other women need to be checked on more than your own kids." Mom trails his heels all the way from the kitchen to the living room.

"Oh yeah? Well maybe other women appreciate me more."

Dad grabs his keys and his coat.

Shivers tingle up from my belly as Mom scans the coffee table for something to fling at my Dad's head. An Elton John record album. The disc whizzes overhead, shattering against the wall, meaning those great songs will no longer sing from our speakers.

"Mom, Dad, STOP!"

I *hate* when my parents break our things. We already don't have enough. I don't get why anyone would smash their own things, knowing full well they're going to be impossible to fix later. If I hug my body tight, pinch my eyes shut, and hold my breath maybe I can reverse time.

"Don't you dare walk out of this house!"

Mom unplugs our glass table lamp and smashes it against the front doorknob just as Dad's reaching for it. There's something about the idea of having broken music and a knocked out light in the doorway of my house that says emergency to me. It calls for screaming sirens. I want ten deafening alarms to fill the air of my neighborhood, red lights flashing all the way to my house. A pageant of nurses in white will carry me out on a great big stretcher, shocking my parents into silence. They will finally realize that I am exactly as crushed as the broken lamp and as silenced as the music lying scattered and sharp on our living room floor.

When you know nobody's coming to rescue you from your confusing life, you can't do much except wonder how fast you're falling and how hard you'll land. If we run for it now we'll make it upstairs before we see something we really don't want to see. Then all we'll have to fret over is hearing something we don't want to hear. The kind of talk that soils your good memories until you forget you had any at all.

Ducking swear words and dodging finger pointing we fling ourselves around the stairway banister and up toward our room. My levelheaded older sister dashes with me in an unusually clumsy way. Toni's shifting bumbling trot makes me worry. She's often the most balanced one of all of us in situations like this.

"Close the door," I tell Toni.

Clack. She snaps our bedroom door in place.

Taking our usual spots beside each other on the bed, we wait for the battle to end. My Sesame Street glow-clock says it's time for the Pink Panther special to come on TV. It's the one thing I was looking so forward to all week.

"I'll be back," I tell Toni, already turning the doorknob. At eight years old, Toni is usually too bossy to agree with anything I say, but tonight she watches me go without a single question.

Walking back downstairs feels pretty safe with the soft support of my teddy bear. He helps me turn on the TV. We'll watch the Pink Panther show together. Teddy likes cartoons, too.

"Go to your room Jenna."

If Mom can sense the TV coming on all the way from the kitchen, you'd think she'd be alerted to my obvious desperation and allow me a few minutes of enjoyment. I spin the small silver dial in a panic to find the cartoon. There's a close-up of the Pink Panther's face on the screen. He's raising his eyebrows like he's done something really smart.

Mom's hands lightly clamp around by my shoulders, physically turning me back in the direction of the stairs.

"But you promised I could watch it," I dispute, pivoting back towards the TV. The cartoon is my only hope for temporary gladness. It works the same as music. If I can feel the good of the Pink Panther it will cancel out the bad inside my house. With a strong arm I deliberately push my Mom's hip aside, pointing to the panther's funny black sunglasses.

"Ha ha, look!" I squeal with dramatic glee.

"Jenna. Now."

"But Dad!"

When Dad pretends not to hear me I pledge to go back up to my room and never come out.

• • •

The middle of the night is the quietest time. It's now long after the fighting. But my heart still pounds like it shouldn't when your body is trying to sleep. These wakeful hours of darkness might feel terribly long if I didn't see my sleeping sister in the bed beside mine and feel this soft pillow against my cheek. There's something about the calm in the late night sky outside my window that says everything isn't always as bad as it seems.

On the way to the toilet I stop to look in the bathroom mirror to see if it's really still me standing there. Staring into my own eyes is the only way to guess how it feels to have someone looking back at me without trying to look away. Sometimes I wish that one day I'll wake up having a calm life and a meaningful place in the world. And sometimes I just wish I won't wake up at all.

• • •

The morning sun is as bright as the Olympic torch, a beautiful thing. Its whiteness bleaches out the salty stains from last night's tears. My Dad says the Olympic torch takes people to a wonderful place called Victory.

The beaming ray of morning sun makes it easy to picture what it's like to live in Victory. The vision affords me the confidence to tell my sister my deepest secret. When I have a problem I always tell Toni because she's as smart as any adult I know. Plus she's the one person on the planet who's the most like me. She sees the same things I see. From a similar height and from the same exact house.

What worries me about telling her this secret is that her sensible nature needs physical proof to believe in uttered admissions. Her requests for explanation force me to doubt myself, wondering why nobody else I know can literally feel what people are thinking and and also see what mistakes they're making before they make them.

"I can feel it."

I spill the beans inaudibly as a practice run.

"What?"

"The whole world. I can *feel* it and it doesn't feel right. I mean, do you ever feel like you're in the wrong place?"

"Yeah, but I didn't know how to tell anybody."

When Toni genuinely turns toward me, my heart feels instantly tingly and warm like there's a peppermint patty melting inside it. I never thought she'd understand.

"Psych! Just kidding," she laughs. "What do you mean 'wrong place?' You want to switch beds?"

"I—I—I um…just don't know how…"

I try to reword my question, but she's already flung her covers off and jumped out of bed to get her day started.

"...yeah, uhnn humph." I decide to just agree with her, realizing that she isn't bothered with figuring out how to live. She actually feels like part of our family. And she seems just fine with the world. Toni rolls her eyes, snatches my teddy bear and tosses it next to my pillow.

"We'll have to switch beds later. It's time for breakfast right now. C'mon. "

The light buttered cloud of hotcake steam rises up to meet us exactly halfway down the staircase. Having pancakes for breakfast means Mom and Dad have already made up. Now I won't have to exhaust my energy trying to make everyone get along. The relief from that knowledge lets me take a full calming belly breath.

"You'd better not ruin breakfast by bringing up the broken record or the Pink Panther special!" Toni feels the need to remind me of obvious things.

"I won't, you id…" Missing the chance to insult my sister, I slip on a step. Toni's right there to catch my fall, but she opts to bend away instead as if my plunge is contagious. So I tumble.

"Good morning, kiddos!"

Dad's welcome comes from behind the newspaper he's reading at the dining room table. His voice is chipper. I guess it doesn't occur to him to ask who just fell down the steps. Toni runs into the kitchen to help Mom. My task is pulling out the heavy oak chair beside Dad and sliding my bruised behind on board. Mom sashays into the dining room armed with hot pancakes, cold Aunt Jemima syrup and hard butter.

"Pass the pink panther cakes...I mean the pancakes," I say discomposed and flushed. How did I let the prohibited words slip out? Toni smirks at me with her freckled lips, rolling her eyes at my flub.

The pancakes and syrup hide the fancy pattern of the blue china plates that Mom and Dad haven't thrown at each other yet. During the days after Mom and Dad fight, I usually get the feeling of having rubber bands strapped all around my head. Today it's more like the elastic is stretching down and around my heart. There's got to be a spell or a magic word I could say to make my parents stay good with each other from now on.

Meals aren't exactly the prime occasions to meditate for solutions though. They're times that make you lose your determined focus altogether, singly due to my sister who takes every stint at the table as a cue to talk nonstop until the last of us has escaped the dining room. She tells greatly detailed but entirely pointless stories about everything in the world she's ever seen or done.

Her meaningless words clutter my brain at an inconceivable pace, but I can't waste my food, so I sit through the whole meal making loud cutting sounds with my fork and knife, chopping up her words and chewing my pancakes. I don't know how much attention Toni needs from Mom and Dad, but I know I need more than she does. So I'll avoid eye contact altogether until she senses it's another person's turn to talk. The plan works against me unfortunately. Ignoring her only makes her talk louder.

"...my friend Tanya has this metal bracelet that has all these things hanging off it like mini cars and high heels and hearts, and it's really cool except it got caught in her hair Friday, which was in this really weird ponytail on side of her head and they couldn't get it out, so..."

The stress of processing so much information at once makes my blood pump wearily. Escape seems necessary. I hurry through the rest of my meal until all that's finally left on my plate is a sticky puddle of syrup.

Mom and Dad finish at the same time I do. The three of us wipe our faces with the napkins Dad brought home from the cafeteria at the State Building where he works for the Governor's Energy Council. His job is to make it so there's enough gasoline and electricity and such to go around.

I try not to get syrup on the three ring pattern part of my napkin because Dad once told me that emblem helps the public stay educated on the benefits of nuclear energy. I lay the helpful napkin on my plate nuclear symbol side up to display it one last time in respect for its good purpose for the people.

The high-pitched sound of chairs sliding on the floor, wood against wood, sends my senses to the ceiling. Luckily, stinging eardrum overload can be shaken off with a simple head wiggle. It feels significant to recover so quickly and fall back into the fold, retreating behind Mom and Dad into the kitchen to dump off the breakfast dishes.

On weekend mornings after breakfast I like to explore the alleyway behind our house. There's never anybody out there, just parked cars and concrete potholes partially pooled with water.

The white plastic seat on my bicycle holds a perfect crescent of last night's rainwater. I grab the bike's damp handlebars, shoving off, driving forward with my foot, not just gliding. Not pedaling, just scooting. Chugging down the backstreet, I know my problems aren't anywhere just because I've left them temporarily. My swoosh of my foot to the ground pushes that thought away. I escape further from my own reality with each sweeping step.

A tiny beady-eyed mouse lies dead, soft yet rigid, in the middle of the lane. The creature looks unhurt on the outside but I naturally know he's broken on the inside.

Since the dead mouse is in danger out here where cars come in and out I'll have to move him to shelter. Everyone says mice carry diseases, so I lift him onto the foot rest of my bike with two stray twigs. There he goes. Sweet gray fur.

You just have to feel sorry for a mouse having to die on the concrete like that. As consolation, I'll take him for one last ride, pedaling him up the alley and back so he can look up at the sky where I believe animals go when they die, just like people.

Up and down the alley we ride once and then twice more, looking at every detail of the trees overhead, listening to the sounds of outside, wondering how animals live all their lives outdoors, thinking that maybe it's something I should try.

When we finish our ride, it's time to lay him down forever. He'll lie here in the tall grass on the hill just above the alley in his final dry spot where he can be dead in private.

Having just seen death firsthand, I feel that it's only considerate to pedal back home very slowly to honor the life that used to be.

It's time to go back inside to see if anyone mi.
me. Toni's in our bedroom, sitting at the small woode.
table by the window between our single beds. She's cutting
the toes off of all our pairs of socks and making them into
hats for our stuffed animals. The few hats she's made so far
are each original, decorated with glued on buttons, stickers,
and safety pins. They're being modeled by Peggy the
Flamingo, Lippy Lion, and the Checkered Chicken. I spin
around on my heel and head back downstairs, wanting
nothing to do with the trouble Toni's going to be in for
scissoring up our socks.

Dad's friends greet brashly when they come in the
cellar door. It's already time for Dad's Sunday dart game
which I like to be part of if I can help it.

"Where's my Dad?"

Dad's tallest friend Mr. T is drinking beer and
fiddling with the radio dials, which means he might give
me a distracted reply. Mr. T settles on a rock music station,
backs up into me, turns toward the dart board, and forgets
my question altogether, keeping focus on the bulls-eye.

"Hey careful you're not in the line of fire, sweetie."

The only line of fire I see is an occasional match
flaring up cigarette tips. I settle into a spot at the high end
of the basement staircase waiting for my Dad to join his
friends in the game.

A cloud of smoke follows me up the steps and
perches above my head like a great haunting ghoul. It's
lurking existence sends me into that funk again, that grey
mood that floods me with feelings much too big to
shoulder all by myself. My escalating emotions linger and
hover until they sting like the dry gas of lit cigarettes. Sad

deep thoughts, broken records, lost victory, tense
ancelled cartoons, scarce attention. I can't deny it.
's up to one gigantic problem. I can't seem to make
el right no matter what I do.

Holding your breath doesn't keep tears under your skin when they're determined to spill. The water dots the stairs, *plunk, plunk, plunk*; steady, like rain. My hands instinctively cuff my eyes for safe cover and soft comfort. An out breath sets more sadness free. Mr. T. turns up the radio to hear his favorite band.

I keep my hands over my eyes.

And make myself stop crying.

By just listening to the music.

Above the chatter of my Dad's dart game buddies, I can make out the words of the song that's on. The band is singing what I know for sure is a message meant specifically for me. They sing.

Hang on. Help is on its way, I'll be there as fast as I can.

My Dad enters the room just then, loitering with his friends, aiming to toss a small dart. As quickly as that I feel hopeful again. I know a sign of luck when it shows up. All I have to do now is just hang on and wait for the help that's coming.

"Yes you can. Just *do* it," I say matter-of-factly. I'm not giving up on my family that easily.

When I see my command isn't working, I try another approach. In my most charming and convincing voice I sing, "I bet I could fix your divorce." I suggest it so sweetly, I think Mom might go for it.

"Nobody can fix this Jenna," she says shaking her head at me, probably not even realizing she just said the four most unbearable words I've ever heard.

Only a few days pass before Dad starts packing up his moving boxes with books and records that belong back where they were on our shelves. I'm trying to stay close to his side for as long as possible before I have to leave for school. As I linger, I take special note of the way his hair curls around his ears and how his shoulders hunch forward ever so slightly even when he stands up straight.

I will do anything if you stay. I can't seem to say the words out loud, but maybe he'll hear my thoughts.

"Hurry up and get dressed for school Jenna," Mom alerts me. "Toni's already ready."

"I can see that," I say smartly. She's eating breakfast in the dining room. How Toni can eat at a time like this is a mystery to me.

"Listen to your Mom," Dad says, shuffling by me, dropping a box by the door. He gives me a poke in the belly which usually makes me laugh, but not this time.

I trip up the stairs to my bedroom, yanking down the first thing I see from my closet, a brown and blue plaid dress. Whipping the polyester garment over my head makes my hair snap and stand up with static. I'm rushing too fast, but I don't dare slow down for fear of wasting precious time that I could be spending with Dad.

In my haste to dress fast, my right foot punches through the worn toe of my navy blue knee sock, costing me the time it takes to make a quick fix; a knot tied at the tip of the sock. The knotted sock will come up a bit lower on my calf than the other, but that's no bother. Squeezing the knot into my shoe is no big deal, either. I'll just pull it out through the last band of my sandal.

Time's up. It's time to go.

"Now get going or you'll be late for school," Mom says, sending each of us off with one brown paper bag lunch. There's something lumpy and heavy weighing on the bottom of mine.

"Give your Daddy a kiss goodbye."

Instead of saying goodbye to my Dad, I decide to leave him just like he's leaving me-to show him how bad it feels having someone you love disappear on you. I run straight past him out of the house and scramble down our concrete porch steps as fast as I can to escape the awful thing I did to him.

The misery I'm trying to dump on my Dad just clings to me tighter. It tugs at my insides, beckoning me to go back and have that last hug and kiss goodbye. I won't go back, though. He has to understand how bad this feels.

And so I walk in step with Toni, away from our hopelessly broken house with a great painful pulling in my body, desperate for things to go back the way they once were; family dinners, bedtime stories, and even broken records.

With our lunch bags and books in hand, Toni and I tackle our usual walk under the brilliant yellow trees, up the two blocks to her bus stop at my school. It's hard to pay attention to the yellow leaves falling on the sidewalk like I did last year. They no longer make me think of golden paths to wonderful places.

I know that a perfect layer of nature once existed directly under the pavement beneath us. I wonder what it was like to live here before the city came. It probably looked a lot like the land on the low mountains we have outside our city of Riverston. There was probably a time where rainfall soaked deep into the forests and fields and meadows right here on my street and pelted the backs of foraging bears, raccoons and deer. Now the rain just washes garbage, tires and grit from the downtown core up the county shore by way of our grubby river.

Toni takes a tight hold of my hand, knowing she's the only friend I have, but she eventually has to let go to climb onboard her bus. She takes a seat nearest a window where I can still stand by her from the curb until the bus leaves. My reflection in Toni's bus window looks small and flat. The bus kicks an inch, hinting that it's about to sweep across the city.

I wave her goodbye. She waves back at me from her little square window, showing me that my honest actions sometimes do get honest reactions. I like that about my sister. She's almost always reacted to me, proof that I'm not completely invisible.

The yellow bus roars off down the leaf scattered road. Saying goodbye to my sister today gives me an incredible urge to run around my schoolyard and yell "hello" at the top of my lungs, because that's the word I want to be saying, not goodbye. I'd never holler like that, though, because people would know I've gone crazy. Instead I calmly walk past clusters of kids who swarm and hover around the doors of my school.

Being the first inside my classroom gives me time to feel good about the room while it's still quiet. When I can drum up good feelings about a room, I find I can stand to be in it longer. Alone at my desk, I pull out a book to act like I'm reading. Nobody in the world would ever suspect that what I'm really doing is trying to figure out what I'm going to do to get through this day. But then again if I can read stranger's feelings really easily, maybe someone will read mine and escort me out of class.

"I guess your classmate Jenna is more interested in the windows than the chalkboard," my third grade teacher says fifteen minutes into first period, making my classmates giggle. I scratch my head and straighten my desk when I realize she's talking about me.

Mrs. Root is tall for a woman. She sticks out her chest when she walks, sending her white person's afro and extra big tinted glasses tilting slightly backward. Sometimes she stops in the middle of teaching to tell really funny personal stories to us like we're her friends, but once we really get to laughing she gets mean and all of a sudden we get yelled at for laughing, and so I guess the joke is on us. But lately, she's been telling fewer stories about herself and making me the joke instead.

"Stop sitting there with your mouth hanging open," she says, even though I've turned my head back to the chalkboard. She catches me with my mouth open all the time. I never notice when I do it. Closing my mouth, I fix my eyes back out the window, wondering what it would be like to be air.

"Stop staring out the window. The front of the room is up here."

The more Mrs. Root tells me to pay attention, the less I find I can. It's hard for me to find the front of the room when my mind is back at home. It's almost the end of the school day, and Mrs. Root still hasn't let up.

"What word did I just teach the class, Miss Jenna?"

She says "Miss" in a snotty way, like I think I'm too good for the class or something. She points to the word SPECTACLES on the board using a wooden pointer with a rubber tip.

thunk.

"C'mon Jenna, what's the definition?"

"Glasses," I say. That one was easy.

I half expected her to be proud or impressed that I knew the answer so she would get off my back, but it only makes her mad. She asks me what a harder word means.

"Define the word *conquer*," she says, tapping her foot, arms crossed, smiling sideways.

The class seems to triple in size when each and every third grader turns to gape at me from their steel desks. I want to tell Mrs. Root that it's *their* mouths that are hanging open this time.

"Close your mouths!" I want to shout at my classmates like Mrs. Root does, to put the pressure back on them.

"Well?" she says.

I think up a big fat blank even though I know this one. It's something to do with a history book. I've seen the word before a ton of times. But I hate history so even if I did know, I wouldn't want to.

"I don't know," I say.

"To beat out, win over or destroy," she says and so she's got me.

After school Mom is waiting out front by Toni's bus stop to take us for a surprise treat at the city mall. We all like the mall because it makes us forget. It makes us forget that we don't have enough. It makes us forget how little there is to do in my city. And it makes us forget about how hard it is sometimes being home together.

"Toni, Jenna, you girls go down to the pizzeria. You can each get a Sicilian slice and a soda," she says, locking up the car in the mall lot. Then pointing, she says, "I'm going to be in that store right over there in the perfume section."

The pizza man shoves a giant red and white triangle of grease under my nose, making me smile big for the very first time today. Steaming grease and sauce is soaking through the paper plate. Gobs of cheese dangle off the ends. I take it in my open palms and lift it up over my mouth, sucking down the overhang. It tastes like bliss, even better than Crèmesickles.

I lean over the rings of water and circles of crumbs on our table to grab the aluminum capped condiment jars, focused on getting the most out of Mom's dollar. I sprinkle almost the whole cheese jar and then about ten shakes of red pepper flakes on my slice. It's not until I finish off the whole slice that my mouth really begins to burn from the red pepper.

"What's wrong with your eyes?" Toni says on our way to the garbage. I notice she has crumbs on her arms and elbows. I don't know why I don't tell her. I just dust off my own.

"I'm just hot from the free red pepper flakes," I say, feeling proud of my thriftiness, blowing my nose into a napkin.

Mom made it seem so easy to find her in the store with the perfume section, but all I can see is a bunch of ladies in white cotton coats and gloves. Aiming smoky glass bottles at passersby, the gloved women spray one person, then another before any of them can say 'no'. It doesn't look like perfume is very safe for your skin since they have to use gloves just to spray it.

Safe.

How is Dad doing without us?

He has to have left work by now, so I guess he's going back to his new empty apartment.

How can this be happening?

Where's my Mom? She's not in sight.

My hands cup my face instinctively in the presence of the white coated ladies. I don't want what they're pushing. Toni sticks out her wrists for a squirt, then treks clear across the store looking for Mom.

Pressing my face against the clean glass countertops of the perfume display is the most soothing way to pass the time until Mom is found. How beautifully the bright white lights shine down on neat rows of colored fragrance boxes. It's so simple and orderly in there. I wish the whole world was like that. Everything would have its place, including me.

A pile of little brown things sit in white bowls by the tester perfumes on the counter. They look like rabbit poop so I don't touch them. Why would someone put animal turds next to fragrance bottles they're trying to sell? It's a mystery to me, but that's not my problem.

All the bottles on the countertop shimmer like jewels. My favorite is the gold bottle shaped like Aladdin's lamp. Grasping it with both hands, I check if anybody's watching, then rub the sides at once, being careful not to drop it.

I wish everything in the world was completely fixed.

The genie doesn't come out in a puff of smoke. So it will have to be freed with a spritz to my wrist.

Your wish is my command.

Snnff.

Aladdin's genie water smells funny. But it would be bad luck to wash the wish off. Maybe my wish could still get granted if I add a squirt of this purple perfume right here.

Snnff. Snnff.

Nope.

Or what about this one.

Snnff.

Or that one.

Snnff.

The cash register nearest me dings and chatters. I can bet any money it's Mom, even though I can't say for sure because I'm having trouble seeing due to this sharp pain stabbing at my left temple.

"Hey Mom," I call out to alert her, snaking my way around all the dazzling countertops to her side. "My head hurts bad."

I swish spit around my mouth to get rid of the metallic perfume taste. It reminds me of the smell of those rusty chains at my school playground. Toni is at Mom's right side watching her burrow through her purse for a wallet.

"Hey Mom," I say again. Mom shrugs now, too busy exchanging a pile of cash for a handful of small bulky shopping bags. I didn't know she had money like that. She always tells us she doesn't have any.

"I think it's going into my skin," I hiss a whisper to my sister, not wanting to admit to Mom all the perfume I've used. My eyes are still watering, my nose really burns, and I think my words sound slurred.

My body is taking the perfume to be poison. It's always been easy for me to spot danger and it's culprit with the precision of a spy. I can never explain how I know what's coming, but I'm always sure I'm right. In the end, it usually turns out I *was* right, but nobody believes me until the proof is visible.

Now that I know I've been poisoned, I wonder how I might die. Will I start bleeding out my nose? Will my brain swell? My brain is swelling I think.

I touch my mouth to see if I can figure out what's not working right on my head. There's no feeling on my lips. Will my Mom find out that I'm dying in time to save me? I wonder if somebody in the store will help me.

"It's not going into *my* skin and I sprayed on as much as you did."

Toni's voice sounds muffled like I'm holding my ears but I'm not. My breathing, my heartbeat echo loudly between my failing ears.

"Uh oh," I say to myself out loud knowing this is the end.

"My goodness girls, you smell like a perfume factory," Mom says, taking her change from the lady.

"Mom?" I say, leaning hard into the nearest mirror, studying my eyes, my tongue, feeling sicker, and dizzier. "I think I'm going to need to lie down."

"We'll be home soon, Jenna," Mom says, shuffling with her purse.

"Oh my gosh," I whisper to myself, because I'm the only one who understands this feeling. The feeling of needing to be rescued fast before everything goes black.

Step back, everyone.

Did she faint?

Muffled voices float around my recumbent body.

Does she need help getting up?

You're going to get her up?

Maybe she shouldn't get up just yet.

And she should probably see a doctor right away.

It's Toni's face I see when I open my eyes.

I *told* her it was the perfume.

"This one can tend to be a little theatrical," Mom says, dusting off my hair as she sits me up. "She'll probably be fine once we get home. We'll get her a checkup this week just to be sure, though."

Stretched across Mom's back seat, I eye the quickening sky through the rear window. The three of us

46

say nothing as the perfect chance to say everything passes away down the highway headed home.

I can't let what's happening to us go silent.

"Is Dad maybe going to meet us at home to take me to the doctor tonight?"

I don't listen for Mom's doubtful answer. Instead I imagine my Dad will be waiting there. When he drives me to the medical center, I'll tell him I'm sorry I left him this morning without giving him a kiss and hug goodbye.

"I just don't like goodbyes," I'll say.

"Don't worry, pumpkin," he'll answer. "I promise you there will never be another goodbye again. I'm coming home for good."

And just like that, he'll turn the car around to take me home. There will be no reason to see a doctor anymore. Because those certain words from Dad will have been all the cure I needed.

I'm standing next to my sister here at Dad's office at the Governor's Energy Council. The poster behind us is about conserving energy.

4

Safe!
Age 8, 1980

"Can we go now?" Toni and I are petitioning Mom even though we know our entire house has to be "spotless" before we go play.

They never should have invented the word spotless. It's cruel.

"Once you get those smudges off the mirror and put away the dishes, you can."

Mom thinks we're dreamers if we actually believe we can play just for the sake of playing, you know, without *earning* it.

Mom works nine-to-five finding new jobs for people who have been put out of work by some kind of horrible accident or sickness. They might have broken their backs or lost a hand or they may have a disease that doesn't let them do the same kind of work they used to do. She took the job because she wanted to help people.

"Good news, I found you a job," she says to the sick people.

"I don't want your stinking job," they say, and then they hang up on her.

"They don't want to work because all they want is their disability check," I remember Mom saying to my Dad over dinner one night half a year ago, before their divorce.

"What's a disability check?" I asked.

"It's free money from the government," Mom said.

"Can we get some?" Dad laughed at my question, saying something about standing in line with crutches for the rest of your life.

Mom works hard. I guess that's why she says we need to keep busy, too. There are endless things to be done, she reminds us. And life is not fair, either, she adds. Being prodded with ideas like that, you get this strong sense that you probably should be shoving off doing something that is hard to do, or at the very least doing anything other than sitting at peace feeling happy and relaxed just as you are.

That's put me in the habit of nervously jumping to it and acting like I'm busy and productive every second I'm not sleeping. I wonder sometimes if I have ever felt satisfied to be producing absolutely nothing. I think that would be a very nice feeling if I could feel it.

Toni grabs the Windex with one hand and lifts a sheet of old newspaper with another, crumbling it in a ball in a hustle toward the bathroom mirror. I head for the cupboards, two hands doing the work of eight, making those spotless dishes and utensils fly into their proper places.

In under a minute, we're finally free to skip down the cracked sidewalk away from our house. I spin under the canopy of oak trees that long ago promised to guard me from everything that could possibly go wrong in my future. Toni does cartwheels.

How easy and comforting it feels to make that two block walk under this harmless stretch of shelter and protection.

Where the canopy opens up toward my school, I get that exciting glimpse of the campus' empty playground.

It's so vacant that it seems awkward or needy, like it's hoping for kids just like me and Toni to fill it up with laughs and play or just plain life.

"Race ya!" I call to Toni. The pace of my happy heart beats double time over the tick, tock of our red steel alarm clock. We always keep it wound, set and close with us so its metallic brrrring will have us home precisely as promised, just in time for lunch.

Racing through the gate, over the blacktop, and past the white painted foursquare and hopscotch spots, we spring onto two black rubber swings. As if part of the same machine, we carve out the air with our toes pointed forward. Pumping our feet high, our heads nearly graze the ground with each pitch forward, two swinging pendulums slicing the sky under the whiteness of puff clouds.

We're air-lifted so far above the pavement that our seats skip, cresting above the top bar of the swing set. The chains on our swings go limp for a second before they snap tight again, making the entire swing set frame tilt and wobble within its concrete foundation.

Being so high in the air is as close to having wings as I've ever felt outside of Dad's arms. When I'm this far up in the air, I get to be the bird, the broad branches of the tree, the sun, the moon and the stars all at once, all looking down from on high. It makes my troubles seem smaller, my worries less tremendous, and the "real world" a far away place.

As my momentum slows, my hair stops blowing in my eyes, letting me see a man I didn't see here a minute ago. He's wearing a dark green zippered vest over a gray shirt with a pair of black pants. His knees stilt high from his low sitting position on the edge of the wooden merry-go-round not far from us. His dark eyes remind me of the bad things that can happen to kids when they're dangling out in the open all by themselves.

A stare like his can make you not want to play anymore. With curbed gusto we swing in smaller, more guarded arches, surely thinking the same thoughts of danger and escape, silently together. You hear stories all the time about kids being followed by strange men in their neighborhoods, but it's always just another story until it happens to you.

Mom's always told us to watch out—that it's a simple fact that people are out there trying to get their hands on you. Each time she's said it there's been a tightening of my neck like my throat's getting grabbed. It made me pay attention during our recent school program on "street smarts."

There was some guy on the assembly stage who called himself "a crime expert who learned the hard way." He said you never really know how you're going to react to a crime unless you actually practice your defense in advance. So Toni and I have been practicing our defenses. Lucky for us we get a lot of chances in our neighborhood.

"Let's go!" Toni and I whisper in sync, stopping our swings and flying into coordinated action. Toni heads to the fence to unlatch it for us. I fast walk in the direction of the man to grab our alarm clock. The clock scrapes the ground when I grab it, a sure signal to the man that we're in a hurry to leave.

I blew it. Now he knows we're afraid, and fear is what makes crazy people act even crazier.

The man leaves the playground when we do, turning right when we turn right, then he follows left after us when we turn again.

"Ok, remember what we practiced," Toni says to me looking straight ahead, clasping my arm cleanly without looking where to grab it.

"He's walking faster," she whispers.

No shit, I think, which is something I would never say, but it's the first thing that came to mind because it's the kind of thing they say all the time on TV.

Our footsteps land quicker to the pavement now, bounding to the pace of a jog. The man follows suit. We quicken to a run. My feet smack down on my own fleeing shadow. Acorns and ants crunch under my feet.

Should we run home to where it's safe or should we not run home because then the bad guy will know where we live? We never practiced this part.

It feels best to head back around the corner toward the comfort of my oak tree canopy that leads back home. But up ahead, there's a gate hanging open.

"C'mon," Toni says sliding us into the fenced yard.

Buzz, Buzzzzzzzzzzzzzzz, Buzzzz, Buzz, Buzz.

Urgently I ring the house's doorbell.

"Whatcha doin'?" The scary man's inside the yard now, coming toward our turned backs. His loud words snap and crack, giving me the mental picture of my looming death.

There's no getaway, just doom. It's like Operation Eagle Claw, when President Carter tried to free the hostages in Iran but eight of the rescuers ended up dying instead. That's how it will happen for me and Toni. It will be a failed escape attempt—the merciless slaughter of two sisters who struggled behind a tall wood fence among some family's barbeque, their picnic table, and a pile of scattered and mauled dog toys. It's not how I want my life to end. I want it to be clean and easy and painless.

There is a deafening ticking sound in the air, a brassy metronome tallying the time that's passing as the man looks back and forth at both of us, waiting for one of us to answer him.

Brrrrrrrrinnnnnnnnnnng.

The clock jitters in my hand.

Toni takes advantage of the startling ringing to run toward the street. I follow, darting past the man until we're safe on the public sidewalk where a group of teenagers are hunched in a huddle. Preoccupied by their own cluster of activity, the teens don't seem to notice the man swooping back to give a swift tug on my arm, pinching my wrist with his grip.

"Toni?" I yell, twisting for her help.

But she's already escaped up the street toward our front door.

"I have to get home. It's time for lunch," I tell the man squarely, tugging my arm hard. My teeth mash together with a biting need to get loose. But he doesn't let go.

"Fire!"

I cry out the word *fire* because in our street smarts assembly they said to yell *fire* instead of *help* because when you yell *help*, nobody will come because they're afraid of getting mixed up in your assault. If you yell fire, they'll come running. So I yell it again.

"Fire!"

It works. The teens turn and gape, making the predator take off down the road, his army jacket flapping in the breeze as his threatening presence literally shrinks with distance.

I make haste toward my house still feeling the ghost of the man's grip on my arm. His emotional residue gives me a deep sense of his feelings; mad, lonely, wild, afraid, lost. Running faster works to pry his pained emotion from my senses. I can't let his personal misery get under my skin.

"Jenna!" I recognize my Mom's voice calling me from down the block. Toni must've told her we were being chased.

A sympathetic man rounds the corner ahead of me, stepping onto a square of sidewalk equidistant between myself and my house. He's wearing a crisp white shirt, creased pants and fancy white shoes.

"Miss, stop ya runnin' for a second. I came to help ya," he says.

The man in white appeals to me so loud and so sure that the rest of the world goes away for a second. Even all the grief and suffering left behind by the perpetrator.

"Ya see, little child, I unna-stan." He kneels down to let me know he's not going to chase me.

I stop running, and step one, two, three steps closer to him. He's now one pavement block away. He can't reach me.

"Ya don't need to be afraid..." His eyes are clear–brownish green pupils floating in the middle of bright white eyeballs. The slight wrinkles around his eyes soften and gleam.

And just like that I know I'm safe.

So I stand still for once.

Yes, I stand perfectly still.

Right where I am.

"Jenna!" my Mom calls with a distressed yelp.

"I have to go," I tell the nice man, skipping away swiftly as I can down the sidewalk toward home.

"I'm right here!" I return.

After she hugs me and takes me inside, I can't help but go straight to the front window looking for the man with the kind eyes, hoping he'll walk down the sidewalk by my house. But he never does.

I brood for weeks about what would have happened if I'd have stayed on the sidewalk and talked to him. Should I have run back to him? Why couldn't I have at least stayed long enough to find out exactly what he understands and how he thinks he might help me?

5

The Ten Minute Difference
Two Weeks Later

"How about we go get some things for dinner, chillins?" Dad tilts the last swig of his beer to his lips, steers slowly over the ruts and potholes of the grocery store parking lot.

Poised to earn my worth as the cart pusher I fling myself out of the car to try to beat my sister as the first to snatch us a grocery cart. Toni speeds off to race me to the carts, all bouncing heels and springing curls, kicking her knees up high. The express pace of her red and white checkered sneakers makes it look like she's streaking the air with pink paint. I run close behind her with my hands out forward, ready to give her a push out of the way when I catch her, but she gets to the carts before I get the chance.

The rickety racket of the rolling cart across the parking lot makes me have to plug my ears.

"Toni, push the cart quieter the rest of the way" I say, rubbing away the rattling pain from my tender inner ears with my pinky fingers. She listens and slows down.

The second we get inside the grocery store, I know I can unplug my ears. There's nothing in here that will bother them, just a mellow low toned hum of refrigerated machines and the soft strumming music of John Denver on the sound system. The cart rolls quietly on the smooth waxy floor. It's all the kind of gentle noise that lets me feel like I can stand around for hours if I want and compare olives to my heart's content. That is, if I liked olives, which I definitely don't.

Toni gives Dad full charge of the cart now. He knows the aisles well, which tells me he's been shopping here a lot on his own. I don't like that he has a life away from me, my sister and my Mom. People must think he doesn't belong to anyone when they see him walking around without his wedding ring or his family.

I would get lonely buying eggs, butter and pork chops just for one. Doesn't Dad miss us being a family? It must feel so terrible to be walking around all alone without a family. I mean it is terrible. It is so terrible to be alone.

A cloud of white frost poofs out at my face when Dad opens the door to the frozen foods, making me shove my hands under my armpits for emergency warmth.

"Geez, the air conditioning in this store is up so high it could snow. Aren't you guys cold?" I say through chattering teeth, watching Dad walk to the wings of the frozen chicken section.

"Then go stand outside."

I can barely hear my sister answer from inside one of the other coolers. She's stacking cans of frozen fruit juice to make a dangerously high tower of purple, orange and green containers. I hate being told to go, especially since I'm trying so hard to get my family to want me around in the first place. I look beyond my sister to see if Dad's anywhere in sight. No, he's already moved well beyond us both, coupons in hand, steadfast in his search for the best deal on Cream of Mushroom soup.

Goose bumps raise high like a field of golden wheat on my arms, this time for the chill in my heart. Toni wants me to go and Dad keeps leaving me behind without checking on me. I want them to be sorry for it. I decide to disappear undetected out the aisle, past the magazine and candy racks, beyond the cashiers and out the automatic door into a blanket of natural warmth. They'll worry themselves sick about me, never thinking to look out here.

The outdoor sounds of the banging, jittering carts scour my ears again, echoing painfully deep in my head. I hold my ears and crouch down on the curb in front of the store where the long red fire zone stripes lash out from the building.

Kids as old as me are riding in the back seats of sedans that slow down off the road and circle cautiously into the parking lot, filling in empty spots to complete perfect rows of colored cars. Moms and Dads emerge first, talking to their children, looking in their eyes, guiding them inside, handing them jackets. Jackets! I don't want them to see me sitting here all alone. At the same time I wonder who is ever going to see me.

My stomach gurgles, churns and burns, a warning that there is about to be another bout of diarrhea. This has been happening to me more and more, no matter what food I consume. I have to run to make it to the bathroom. Thank goodness it's right up in front of the store in plain sight.

The doorknob turns, the toilet waits, the door clicks shut behind me. I made it. I'm already going, a steady stream of stink filling the air and the bowl when somebody opens the door. A woman. I didn't have time to lock the door. I cover my privates and she gets a red face and says "oh sorry" and disappears. Unable to get up just yet, I watch the door, thinking about how it still isn't locked, hoping there won't be a second surprise.

My hiney burns hot so I have to pull up my pants very gently. I stroll out of the bathroom with as little strain as possible, trying to turn my focus from the flaming pain by carefully examining the store's product displays, shelf lighting, and aisle signs. With each aisle I pass, I take note of how the sundry details of the store all come together to produce one total shopping experience. Yes, the whole place looks sharper, cleaner, and newer than the store where Toni, Mom and I shop.

I kick a quarter someone dropped on the floor. Looking around to make sure nobody sees me I shove it in my pocket. What luck! It'll buy me a Charleston Chew at the register.

Dad and Toni haven't been searching for me. The two of them are walking together looking at mayonnaise and relish, not even realizing they're pushing someone else's cart down aisle six. My Dad usually does dumb things like that as soon as I'm not around to correct him. Thank goodness I'm back.

"You guys have the wrong cart," I say walking up behind them, hoping they'll turn around and say, "Where have you been? We've been looking all over for you!"

"We have the right cart, Jenna," Dad says, actually answering me. I roll my eyes the second he says it, wondering why people can't just admit their mistakes.

"Dad, look in the cart. We *never* buy these foods!"

Then I realize that I said "we," meaning Mom, not Dad. Having tossed me a small jar of mayonnaise, Dad asks me to put it in the cart. That makes me feel special again. I plop it down beside the four frozen pounds of ground beef.

I pick up the package of meat to study the gray wiggly lines pressing against the tightly stretched plastic. There's pinkish blood all around the edges, leaking onto my hands. Is there blood in our food? The idea of it makes me go white, feeling my behind burning again.

Back to the bathroom I run, this time sure to lock the door. I'm the queen of my seat and I can make all the things I hate about life flush out of my body as fast as my diarrhea. Up until now, they've just been circling in me, not flushing. Piling up, and up, clogging up my works. But this time I've made sure all the dirty wastes have been expelled for good.

• • •

Dad's apartment is peppered with sweet smelling cinnamon candles. They do a good job of canceling out the musty smell of the secondhand furniture. But based on what's in kitchen garbage, we might all be waking up to heavy hints of stale beer, fermented wine corks, and dry ashes.

The bare floors are as clean as his dusted, uncluttered tabletops. Books and albums have been cleanly placed on his homemade brick and wood plank shelves in alphabetical order like Dad taught us—by last name of the singer or by the first letter of the band name, except bands like The Who, which is under W, not T.

His music selection is Elvis Costello, extracted from in between the latest of The Cars and classic Bob Dylan.

Just about the time Dad's first seasoned burger patty starts to sizzle in the bacon grease, Elvis Costello's voice gets caught on the words Peace, Love and Understanding. I race Toni to the stereo, hoping to be the one to save the day by cleaning the fuzz off the record needle.

Toni makes it first, correcting the skip.

I make two fists.

"I fixed it," she yells.

"Thanks, Toni," Dad calls out from the kitchen, meaning Toni wins.

The air already smells like rosemary, the "romantic" smell my Mom practically swoons over when she makes her famous meatballs. I think it smells wonderful, too.

Anticipating a good meal, I pull out a chair intending to park myself at Dad's dining room table. Until I notice that the plastic seat cover is perfectly wrecked. I'm surprised my Dad didn't notice his chair has so many slices and sharp edges. I myself need for chairs to be smooth and perfect.

Maybe I can fix this one before dinner. I press the peeling vinyl down to return it to its rightful place over the yellowing foam.

"Dinner's ready," Dad merrily calls out of the kitchen. I look around for some glue that might happen to be lying around within arm's reach. Or some tape. Tape will work, if it's good tape.

"Dad, do you have any tape?" I can't seem to let go of the vinyl. It will stay fixed as long as I don't stop pressing.

"Come on Jenna have a seatski," Dad says encouragingly.

"But this chair has got to feel like crap to sit on, excuse my language," I say shaking my head at Dad, indicating that I won't sit. I rub my hands to smooth out the deep lines that the vinyl imprinted on my palms.

Dad offers an accepting nod allowing me to stay standing at the table. He scrapes a plastic spatula under one of the burgers delivering a huge, juicy one on my plate. It's already fixed just the way I like it–with lots of cheese, a glob of Hellmann's mayonnaise and no bun.

Dinner tastes so good I forget about Dad's ruined chair and my earlier stints of burning diarrhea. I even second guess my disgust about the gray squiggles and blood from the grocery store meat. Maybe it wasn't as gross as I made it out to be.

From where I stand at the table, my sister is totally hidden behind Dad's massive frame. And I don't know if it's the food or the music but something's keeping her strangely silent. That makes it easy to pretend it's just me and my Dad eating together.

I take full advantage of this time alone with him, taking focused snapshots of him with my mind so I will have a clear mental picture of him to keep once he's died. I study my Dad as he eats, committing his face and hands to memory. I note his fondness for music, good burgers, tall posters, high bookshelves and rising potted ferns.

"I love you, Dad," I say just in case today's the last time I see him alive. It'll be fresh in his mind so he'll remember it on his trip up to heaven.

"I love you, too, kiddo," he answers with a smile, not hesitating.

"I love you three," Toni laughs, coming back into the picture.

• • •

Instead of sleeping, I'm looking up at my Dad's ceiling from his mattress and box spring that are stacked directly on the floorboards. I imagine his bed is really two soft square layers of vanilla cake and his brown sheets are the chocolate icing. The floor is the wooden plate. Toni's asleep on her slice.

Dad's snoring from the couch in the living room. Not me. The red monster is making me restless. This monster comes to me anytime of the day lately, but mostly when I'm by myself. His crimson fur frame vibrates with a madness that stirs up all the bewildered thoughts that have settled down deep in the crevices of my brain.

The red monster confirms all my fears. He talks about them when I'm awake and he reminds me again of them in my nightmares. I can feel him coming right now and I don't think I can stop him.

"Your Dad is going to die!" His giant frame shimmies and quakes like a furious fire when he says it. And of course I believe him, because I have already felt this truth in my gut like the strongest, most dreadful hunch.

My Dad is definitely going to die.

It makes me fear that maybe I have the power to predict the future through potent feelings that come to me in the night. I don't want any more pictures to come. There's a great fear of what they might tell me about my family's future.

• • •

When Dad sneezes from the couch, it tells me he's awake and still alive. On tenterhooks for the privilege of talking to him alone, I inch my toes out of bed to keep from waking my sister. Gently closing the bedroom door I plod out to the kitchen where coffee percolates.

My ears are ringing from the party Dad took us to last night. The adults blasted the music so loud that after a few hours of playing and eating all I wanted in the world was complete dead silence and a normal night's sleep. So I asked for it.

"Dad, can we go now?"

"Huh?"

"Can we go?"

"Go?"

"Yeah."

"Go where?"

"Home."

"Home?"

I rolled my eyes and gave up, feeling unguarded and stuck. Hanging around smoke, loud music and even louder people way past my bedtime felt like sensory excess.

Noticing Toni was pleasantly busy with other kids in the TV room, I searched alone for the makings of some kind of cocoon to protect myself from all the commotion. It didn't take long to find a dark bedroom where we had put our jackets earlier. I dug mine out and put it on so I'd be ready to leave the second Dad said "let's go."

Now what to do? Bored, but too wired up to sleep, I crawled onto the bed, burying myself under the large pile of coats and pocketbooks. I waited there listening for Dad for hours, hearing nothing but muffled music and cackling voices. I worried about how if I yelled for help for whatever reason, no one would hear me.

The coffee smells ready.

"Good morning Dad. Can I have some?"

When I ask him for something and he gives it to me we share a closeness that I like. I know by now Dad would never say no to me when it comes to adult things like beer or coffee because he doesn't want me to feel any less than an adult. I don't ask him for anything like money or dessert, though, because he would say "sorry we don't have any". I couldn't bear that rejection.

Coffee turns out to be the grossest thing I've ever tasted. I make myself drink half the cup to prove I can. You look pretty important to be holding hot coffee in your hands, the black liquid sending curls of steam whirling out of the mug.

"I'm going out to play."

I hear Toni's announcement before I even see her. She's already dressed and reaching for the door, skipping breakfast. That makes me want to follow her outside. My drink's steam has given itself over to room temperature anyway, so the magic is gone.

"Bye, Dad," I leave my cup to join Toni.

My Dad's apartment complex is for adults only, so there's no playground for kids. But being outside on a flat lawn can be playground enough if you just use your imagination. I myself could spend hours just fiddling around in the grass picking clovers and watching bees pack dandelion pollen onto yellow lumps on their tiny back legs.

Toni's climbing a tree by the far parking lot. I'm too wrapped up in the fragrance of the nearby lilac bush to follow her. Lost in the beauty of my favorite flowers, it takes me a minute to notice Dad's come outside with his camera focused on me. Leaning into the lavender blooms, I can feel the bottoms of my pants rise to show I have no socks on. They've teased me for it at school, so even though it's only Dad who's looking, I reset my stance to hide my bare ankles.

"Smile kiddo!"

Dad's direct words startle me. I manage a sunshine generated squint. The camera is the only thing that gets Dad looking directly at his girls and no one else. I'm sure that's why Toni's headed our way right now, talking a mile a minute, aiming to compete for this sparse dose of attention.

"Dad, Dad, what are you taking a picture of?"

Toni saddles up beside us, already babbling in a quick tempo. "Last week this kid Henry was caught taking pictures in the girls' bathroom at school and he got his camera taken away from him and some people said they developed the film and the pictures were just black anyway because he left the lens cap on. Isn't that dumb? Boy, Henry is so dumb…"

"Quit talking so much, you big fat blabbermouth," I spout. "You never leave a second to let me say anything."

I didn't plan on saying that exactly, but you can't always plan out your feelings. Sometimes they just come up because you're feeling like a match on flint.

"That's because you don't have anything to say!"

"Yes, I do."

"Then go ahead, say something."

The truth is there are things I want so desperately to talk about, but some things I'm realizing there are no words for. Watching the world fall apart on the news makes you teeter where you stand. Usually you'd fall back on your family if it weren't itself in for repairs. After years of seeing evidence of how nothing's working you just can't stop your heart from aching. Even though I'm dying to talk about it all, the descriptives are missing from my language.

Toni folds her arms and waits, looking directly at me. She seems very pleased with herself. I wonder how pleased she's going to be when she's bald from me pulling all her hair out.

Dad aims his camera on the both of us, ready to shoot, and that makes me feel like the whole world is watching our stupid conversation. Toni is trying to make me sound dumb. My temper bubbles up but I cool it off quick by sniffing the flowering lilac bushes.

If I were a lilac flower, I think, *I would never have to say a thing. People would gather around me and I would remind them how great the silent things are.*

"See, I told you. You have nothing to say," my sister says, proving that she's the biggest jerk alive.

"Dad, would you tell Toni to shut up?" I whine.

He doesn't answer. And so Toni keeps talking.

I make my way around to the far side of the lilac bush, where the building's fan unit blows hot air away from the brick building, thankfully drowning out my sister's nonsense.

I inch as deeply as I can into the center of the bush until I'm surrounded by branches, leaves and flowers. It feels like a hug from the earth, clean and pure and fun.

"If you have a problem, you're going to have to learn to cope."

Toni's breaking whole branches off the lilac bush to get to me.

"Don't break the branches, geez!" I say, already brainstorming ways I can keep Toni's broken branches alive in a vase in Dad's apartment. She listens, now merely bending the branches back.

"What's cope, anyway?" I ask her through the thin thicket, wondering if "cope" is the solution I've been waiting all my life for.

"Everybody knows what *cope* means. It means act like you don't care. Duh!" She proceeds to fling the branches back into my face before following Dad back inside.

By the time I come back in, Dad's made a few little white cigarettes with sheets of thin square white paper. But they don't look like the ones you buy in stores. They have pointed tips and a fat middle. I know this kind of cigarette from a drug commercial that says they're against the law. My Dad could go to jail if somebody sees him and reports him. Somebody like me.

My eyes dart nervously between my Dad and the phone. Where's Toni? She knows what I know–about calling 911 to turn criminals in. We learned it's the right thing to do. It's morally wrong to keep a secret from the police.

The toilet flushes, telling me Toni will be out here in a minute to instruct me.

It turns out Dad's been keeping the filler for these cigarettes hidden in black plastic canisters meant for camera film. He sprinkles a canister's contents on a thin square of cigarette paper.

I consider my options.

Toni's most recent advice was to cope–to act like I don't care. But minds and hearts like mine don't let you pretend. Shamarra called it being authenic, which sounds friendly and poetic.

Where *is* she?

I can't hold it in any more.

"You can go to jail for that, you know," I warn my Dad loud enough for him to hear me over the TV.

"Huh?"

Dad answers directly to the TV, not to me. His voice is dull, not alerted in the least. A metallic sounding flick on the wheel of his yellow plastic BIC lighter, sparks a flame that burns the tip of his freshly rolled cigarette. The tip glows when he pulls air through it with his mouth.

My lips tighten at the same time his do.

He holds his breath.

I hold mine.

At last, the smoke rolls out through his nose and teeth. His body folds back in, slumping down. The smoke he breathes out smells better than cigarette smoke. And it doesn't burn my eyes. But it does something to his. It makes them look closer to cat's eyes now–narrow and glossy. The dull sheen in his gaze feels like when the bathroom mirror fogs up and you disappear. Dad might be sitting right near me, but his blank look tells me his attention's gone again. He made his eyes say goodbye before I got a chance to prepare for them to go. Now I know firsthand why the law made drugs illegal. Because they steal people.

The taste of the morning's black coffee is back in my mouth again. I retreat to the bathroom just as Toni comes out. Without a word to her I shut the door and inspect my mouth in the mirror, searching for the source of the bitterness. I don't find anything.

The Sunday night drive back home to Mom's only takes ten minutes, but the difference between life at my Dad's house and my Mom's is hundreds of miles apart. Mom greets us at the door, grimaces at Dad, and tells us to go straight back to our room. I wonder if Mom knows about the loud party and the fat cigarettes. Maybe she has an idea of what she should do. Surely she'll take care of it.

Nobody's going to take care of anything.

The volume of my worries turns up loud as I climb into bed later on in the night. With a click-click of the switch on my nightstand lamp, I make our bedroom pitch dark, a black welcome mat for that horrible red monster.

"Goodnight Toni," I say needing to hear my own voice out loud so the monster thinks I'm not alone. But he's not fooled. He knows my sister is already sound asleep.

He's brought some multicolored friends this time, a rainbow of spooks threatening to shake me off my center right in my very own bed. They chant, "Nobody's going to take care of anything" with mounting voices. The fiends get a laugh out of that.

I pull up the covers to hide, but they show up even bolder and brighter and they hoot even louder, now a hundred howling faces lined up in perfect rows across my closed eyelids–just daring me to make them go away.

6

What It Feels Like to Be Air
Six Months Later

Mom makes us stay home a lot of the time and she doesn't want us to make a sound while we're here. That leaves me plenty of time to write poems about how it's a waste of life being silent and bored.

We have to keep our doors open so Mom can listen for the noise she says we're not supposed to make. Her ears are always tuned and ready for any vibration, whisper, or whistle that might fire her up into a fit of fury. Desperate for comforting harmonious melodies, I sometimes put my radio directly up to my ear at volume level one. It's often when my music isn't on that Mom yells from the kitchen that I'd better turn it off.

Thank goodness we found out my Grandma was putting dirty dishes in her apartment cupboard. It made Mom ask her to move in with us. Her social security checks are helping us pay the mortgage. With Grandma in the room between me and Toni, I think I'll be less bored. Maybe I'll even write a poem about Grandma and her dishes.

My Grandma's thin body and black horn-rimmed glasses make her look simultaneously delicate and thorny, like I often feel. My Mom's mom is the widow of a grandfather who left the world way before I joined it. I can't imagine somebody living on the Earth at a different time than me any more than I can envision Grandma ever having been a wife to somebody. Both are just too weird to fathom.

Mom said Grandpa died of a heart attack back when she was still in grade school. The shock of it made something go haywire in Grandma's head.

"It can't be cured," Mom said, which gave me a powerful flash of déjà vu.

You only ever see Grandma in patterned polyester dresses, with the unfinished look of her knee high hose rolled halfway up both calves. Cut short and completely silver, her hairstyle is all curls because of a perm that needs no styling after a shampoo.

Grandma does quite a bit of sitting in her bedroom staring at the wall, with the exception of going to the bathroom and heating up her own soup for lunch. Since all I'm really competing with for Grandma's attention is her wall, I know she'll be thrilled to listen to me talk about my deep thoughts and grand ideas.

"Hello...Grandma?"

I knock at her open door even though I'm already inside her room. She doesn't look up at me. I just saw her standing up a minute ago taking pills from the prescription bottles on her dresser top. Little red and blue ones. I know she can hear me.

She's the one I need to talk to. I've spent all afternoon brainstorming various solutions to all the problems of the world. They're ready to be heard. I don't bother telling Toni about them because she's made it clear that I'm weird for going on about the problems of animals and forests and homeless people when there's nothing I can do about it.

From this perspective just inside Grandma's doorway I can see into Toni's room. She's been working on a massive artistic concoction for hours, a two foot tall striped house made with rolled strands of colored Play-doh. Toni didn't bother to invite me to see her art. So Grandma and I won't bother her with our ideas about saving nature from development and taking war away from the planet.

"Hi Grandma," I say louder this time, moving towards her bed where I can sit and face her. Her soft gray hairdo looks pouffy. Her body posture stays concave. You'd think she'd fallen asleep in her chair but at closer look, she's actually awake and scowling at her lap with open eyes.

"You're not busy."

Grandma hugs her arms around her body, completely cloistered. While I wait for her to say something, I flick bits of lint off of her bedspread. Her lips stay pressed together in a furrow.

Yanking the wad of bubble gum out of my mouth, I roll it between my palms until it forms a perfectly round ball. Chewing the dirty wad a second time is a stale blueberry mistake.

Grandma's *Birds of the City* calendar swings as the central heat switches on, blowing air up from the floor vent. *Pigeons*, it says in big green letters.

"I was thinking about something really neat today. Did you ever see a dead pigeon? I haven't."

I offer as much fervor as I can muster, guessing that Grandma must be interested in pigeons if she's going to look at one on her wall for a whole month.

"Hundreds of them are running around the city, but you never see a dead one, you know? I wonder where they go when they die, don't you? Maybe they only die every hundred years or something. What do you think?"

The central heat switches off, making the room seem extra silent and awkward.

Grandma keeps quiet, her eyes focused on her lap. Now I know what it's like when I clam up when Mom is trying to talk to me. It's just weird. Stretching the blue wad of gum back out of my mouth makes it snap in two. I force the rubbery mass back together by rolling it into a thin wormy log.

"Praise Jesus!"

They're the last two words I would expect Grandma to say. The words explode from her lips like something forced her to say it. She makes eye contact with me for a split second. Then she relaxes, exhaling with this low toned hmmmmmm that is less like breathing and more like she's trying to spook me. It's working. After an even longer spell of dead silence, I twist the gum into a pretend jewel for my ring finger and get up to leave.

On the way past my Grandma, she uncrosses her legs with so much gusto she accidentally kicks my shin with all her might.

"Ouch!"

"Praise Jesus," Grandma blurts a second time, looking straight at me with an untrusting look.

• • •

"Where you goin'?"

Grandma wonders why I'm headed outdoors during the peak of a flash rainstorm. There's no way to explain how warm downpours delight me.

"Don't go far. Your mummy's soon home."

Grandma calls my Mom mummy, and every time she does, I picture my Mother wrapped head to toe in white gauze.

"I'll just be outside, Grandma."

My Grandma must have a passion for predicting and derailing the peak of my excitement. Her pressed lips and clenched jowls make it clear that she disapproves of my forthcoming street gutter bliss. In fact, every time I finally get ready to do something fun, whether it's opening up my Easter Basket, reading a Mad Magazine, or beating my sister at arm wrestling, Grandma appears with a sneer, forecasting that trouble is brewing if I don't stop enjoying myself.

"You'd better hurry back in," Grandma warns.

I never listen to her, though. I'm fed up with my good times always being on a timer, people constantly saying "time's up" on my fun before I'm done. I roll my eyes mockingly at Grandma and keep walking, letting the screen door slam behind me for effect.

Just being barefoot in a cleansing cloudburst lifts my spirits five notches. I relish in the asphalt warmed rainwater rising around my ankles. The storm passes in seconds. Streaming sunlight returns, making the lingering drizzle visible. High speed spillway water tapers back down to a mere trickle.

I comb our wet lawn with curious toes, fishing for spring clover, examining surfacing worms and slugs. In a tangle of crabgrass lies a rare treasure; a small eggshell. Sprawled nearby, a hatchling catches my eye. She's purple and featherless, perfect and lifeless.

I'm fascinated by her new beak, her slick body, those eyeballs that bulge under tightly closed lids. She's much more real than the bird embryos we have floating in jars of formaldehyde on the shelves in science class. Her freshly expired absoluteness makes me look at her in a very devoted way. I imagine how this tiny creature might have looked if she'd been able to grow feathers and fly alive in the sky.

I name her Wonder because she makes me think about life—about what life has to show me and what I'm supposed to think about the things it shows me.

This delicate creature needs to be safely adored for awhile before she gets buried in a nice grave. Leaving her for a moment in the mist, I rush to the kitchen to get a container for her. Inside our cupboard there's a roundish juice glass shaped like the top of a wine goblet without the stem. It's as close to an egg as anything I can find. It will protect her. I grab pieces of silverware; a fork to gently lift the bird's droopy body and a spoon to steady her head. Positioning the bird in the glass exactly right means she'll be lying just like she would have lain in the egg itself.

Post storm sunshine projects a subtle spotlight on the hatchling as I deliver her into the glass. Her sun-polished body glows a faint yellow-orange. Wonder waits in the goblet on the front lawn while I prepare her burial spot out back. The earth is soft from the rain, making it easy to dig an area as wide as my open palm and as deep as two pine cones.

"Hey Mom," I shout from the backyard when I hear her car drive up. I'm excited to show her the body right before I bury it.

"Holy shit, Jenna, what are you doing putting a dead bird in my good glass?" she exclaims as she gets out of the car.

"It's Wonder..." I call, tensing with trepidation for what's about to happen.

From the grave I can see Mom snatching the glass off the ground. I sprint towards her just as she's lifting the lid on the outdoor garbage can to dump Wonder away.

"Don't!" I plead. But it's too late.

Plop.

I've never seen anything worse than Wonder's little purple head falling limp next to soda cans and boxes of instant mashed potatoes like she's a worthless equivalent to the garbage beneath her.

"But Mom, I made her a grave," I say, dropping stiff tears.

Mom's already got the trash bag all bundled up though, not yielding. I follow steadily behind her wondering how people get to the point where they think it's normal to throw a tiny body in the garbage and leave it at the side of the road to be loaded up in junk trucks, like the earth's birds are rubbish just because they're dead.

With a brave swipe, I grab my Mom's arm tight.

"Wonder's in there!"

"Jenna..."

Mom's arm easily resists my clasped hand. But there again, something changes. She sighs. Her eyes roll to the sky in surrender. With a light toss, she deems the garbage bag dumped and ambles into the house.

My heart soars when I find Wonder. She's stretched out across a white pizza box next to Mom's rejected goblet. The box becomes a sturdy cardboard stretcher that I use to carry her with great concentrated concern. It's because I understand she's even frailer now after having been unfairly insulted and so roughly handled. My heart marches ahead of me to the backyard burial ceremony.

I release Wonder from the box into the small hollow I've dug. Before I cover her with ground, I take a moment of silence to lie down in the wet grass and stroke her shiny body.

"Wonder, how is it that I could be born a person and you could be born a bird?"

Her head shifts ever so slightly when I straighten her feet.

"And why would a bird as pretty as you live just long enough to hatch from an egg and then still die?"

I can wonder all I want I guess. But the truth is there are some questions about life that just don't offer easy answers.

I cup my hands into scoops, bulldozing an ample pile of dirt on top of the animal's body. Once the ground on top of Wonder's grave is patted down flat, I mark it with her broken eggshell, feeling particularly close to the true center of my heart.

7

Secret Thoughts
Age 9, Spring 1980

Leaning against these cold concrete lunchroom walls is like sitting underwater at the YMCA pool, floating in a fixed square of space that's full of people's heads and legs and arms but barren of any real life. By this time each day, I'm feeling a little hungry for lunch, but what I'm starving for is a little taste of nature. I'm trying to make the best of it by thinking of reasons why standing in the lunch line during the sunniest part of the day could be seen as a good thing. I can only think of one reason. Carlo Calamia.

Carlo is the most alive boy I know. In fact he's the only real piece of nature I can find way down here in the humdrum school cellar. He makes me forget about the troubles in my head in the same way that squirrels and rabbits and the cats in our alley do. Watching him is like looking at an animal from one of those nature shows. He has that glossy dark skin glistening like the coat of a panther that rolls tight against his healthy muscles and sturdy bones.

Carlo moves fast and strong in line just ahead of me. He doesn't shuffle his shoes or dilly dally like the other boys. I fix my eyes on the Campbell Soup Kids poster until I know it's safe to get a glimpse of him while he pays for his meal and accepts his change.

He takes his seat with the pride of a lion at a table full of girls and boys by the far wall of the cafeteria. A streak of sunlight darts between his eyes to his right dimple as he tosses and catches food being traded with three other kids. His perfectly carved fingers curl around to claw his sandwich when he takes the first bite, deepening his dimple.

My lunch tray glows green like a fishbowl under the rows of long bright lights that make the ceiling look like the commercial for Lite Brite. I want to sit at Carlo's table, so I walk in his direction. Instead of sitting, a fit of nervousness makes my feet keep on trekking right past his table and straight towards the wall behind him.

I pretend I meant to walk to the wall, scuttling with my tray along the cafeteria's chilly boundary until I reach the exit door where the sunlight is shining in. Feigning interest in something very important happening outside, I peer out the exit door's cloudy little window. The warmth of the incoming sun flattens the goose bumps on my chilled arms. In the sun, the hue of my lunch tray changes from a fishbowl green to a more natural color, closer to the shade of spring leaves. The color transformation transports me elsewhere temporarily.

"Jenna, take a seat."

The husky female voice of the lunch teacher on duty scares me enough to tweak my nervous reflex, making my applesauce topple over the edge of my tray. My eyes go exactly where I don't want them to go, to Carlo's eyes. Eyes always tell the truth and I'm afraid he'll see that I need to know what he thinks about me being a little bit clumsy.

For a split second we're locked pupil to pupil and I'm showered with tingles, a feeling like I've just caught the gaze of a wildcat. Satisfied by the momentary rush of indoor wildness, I pick up my applesauce, find a seat near some quiet people, and eagerly devour my submarine sandwich.

Today we're having a visit from the two nutrition ladies who show up here once a year looking about as healthy as wilted spinach. They force feed us Juicy Juice, a drink that's all water and fruit skins with no sugar. I've never seen that juice on the shelves at my grocery store and I can see why. Then they ladle out prunes, two to each tray, telling us they make a good dessert and that fiber is the extra surprise bonus.

I have more important things to do than think about fiber. I want to tell the nutrition ladies that prunes are not going to help me fix the problems of the world or save my family. But they never actually talk to us. They just transport crates of disgusting things to our school and tell us to eat them.

The teacher on lunch duty says whoever eats their prunes will get a candy and we know she means one of those hard candies wrapped in red plastic with black dots and a twisted green flare on top to look like a strawberry. Motivated by the rare treat, I dream up a simple scheme to earn it.

Step one is to peel back the two butterfly openings at each end of my empty milk box until the top opens wide like a carp's mouth. Then, with the box between by legs, I "accidentally" drop my prunes on my lap, right into the mouth of the milk box and quickly smash down the lid when no one's looking.

When I do it, the lunch duty teacher walks right toward me, pointing her finger. Without thinking, I throw the evidence off of my lap and onto the floor. It lands with a hollow *clop* right by the teacher's toes.

"Danny, settle down. Don't throw your prunes!" she says, pointing to the kid behind me. As she walks, she accidentally kicks my milk box straight into the wall at the end of the lunchroom. The end of the box pops open.

"Oh," she says scanning our trays, "Who dropped their milk box?" Her eyes stop at mine. I look at my fingernails in a hurry.

"Jenna, is that your milk box on the floor?"

"Uh, no."

"No? But you're the only one without a milk box."

"I mean yes," I say, correcting myself.

"Well go pick it up," she says.

I dart across the room with my tray in hand, suddenly feeling like I'm running for my life. Retrieving the milk box I push ahead of my other classmates who are in line to dump their trays.

"Jenna, wait."

The teacher starts toward me, but I don't listen.

I chuck it all in the garbage and watch with relief as the hidden prunes mix with the piles of garbage all the other kids are tossing in with me.

Clenching my arm, the lunch duty lady guides me aside to look into the garbage can. Her bend produces a very revealing view of her enormous boobs and the crack between them.

"I forgot to check if you'd eaten your prunes, Jenna. Did you?"

"Uh huh," I say it soft without nodding my head yes so if she caught me lying I could say that she just heard me wrong because what I had really said was "Nuh uh."

"Good for you," she says, rewarding me by dropping a single sweet into my hand.

Sucking and crunching on my strawberry candy, I don't wonder for a second if it was worth the stress of lying. I know it was. It was the small success I needed to boost my belief that I can let loose on a bigger lie later.

The plan I have in place is to put the brakes on being bullied by Mrs. Root. I have had it with her class time pressures, hassles and harassments. She doesn't realize how badly I need a pouch of security that shelters my raw and overburdened nervous system. You get worn down after coming face to face with neighborhood predators, red monsters, catatonic relatives, unprepared parents and rotten teachers for years without any guidance to show you what it all means. You start to give up on wanting someone to help you. Instead you begin to *need* help in almost a desperate way. So you start to help yourself in ways that other people might not approve of.

Today, I'm not worried about consequences. I just am relieved to know my schoolhouse escape awaits.

I'm usually the last one back at my desk after lunch, but this time I'm the first, keeping my nervousness in check by fishing around the inside of my metal desk for things to fiddle with until the bell rings. I feel my way to a calculator where I can grate my fingertips up and down the buttons to soothe my stress. When the clanging of the class bell sounds, I don't hesitate. I march fearlessly up to Mrs.

Root's desk and tell her very sincerely that I have a doctor's appointment to go to this very afternoon.

"My Mom said she would pick me up in front of the school right after lunch," I say.

"Well then you'd better get out there," Mrs. Root says.

If I knew it was this easy walk right out of school I would have done it the very first day Mrs. Root told me to shut my mouth.

I gallop down the stairs in front of the school, feeling right at home with the sunny outdoors, where school should be held all the time. The fresh air freedom has me feeling spunky, like a kid should. I pick up to a run, bouncing past people who are raking leaves and getting groceries out of their cars.

Yanking the yarn around my collarbone, I fetch a warm key out of my shirt. The bolt unsnaps, telling me with a friendly click that I've broken the last barrier to the peace of mind I am about to enjoy in the privacy of my own house.

Now that Grandma lives with us, Toni and I can go home straight after school and use our house keys to let ourselves inside. That means I don't have to breathe in the rank air inside strange babysitter's houses anymore.

Our first babysitter's house didn't stink exactly. Or at least I don't think it did, but then I can't be too sure because I lost my sense of smell the second the short bald man opened the door to let in all the kids.

Breathing in that house was like inhaling powdered bone dust up your nose. If there was any air in there, it was too weighted down by grit to make it all the way into your lungs. That chalky air sent me into a record breaking sneezing fit that I've never topped before or since. The only thing that got me to stop sneezing was my fear of the sitter man. He delivered all sixteen of us neighborhood kids down to his carpeted basement.

"Why are we going to the basement? It's dark down there," I asked.

"You're going to sleep for two hours," the man ordered, making us all pass under the bridge of his leaning arm.

Not wanting to chance brushing his arm with my head, I did a limbo underneath it. I recently learned the benefits of avoiding the touch of creepy strangers. It's because as I've gotten older, I've noticed that people's blood pulses carry strong impulses. You don't realize it, but every person's palms and skin actually sweat with opinions, beliefs, and points of view that smear all over us like butter when their skin touches ours. Most people don't pick up on it, but I can interpret each touch as accurately as a glass stethoscope. It gives me goose bumps just thinking about it.

"Lie down on the rug."

The sitter called down the shadowy stairs as the first kids reached the cellar. "You can all fit on the floor if you squeeze close together into one long row." And we actually managed to do it, with the open door at the top of the steps projecting a beam of light down, which probably made us look like maggots wriggling around on the floor under the weak glow of a flashlight beam.

Being the one who normally happens to be the first to complain about how I feel, I was ready to speak up and say I wasn't tired—that I wanted to play outside in the sunshine. But that was before the hairless sitter man said with a shout, "Go to sleep or else," and slammed the door with a boom that made me think I might never walk back up the stairs and out of that basement alive.

It's hard to fall asleep when you're lined up smack in the middle of a long string of strange kids lying flat on the floor in somebody's dark basement. That freaky TIME magazine cover came to mind that afternoon, the one about how Jim Jones ordered 913 members of the People's Temple cult to lie side by side, drink grape Kool-Aid mixed with poison cyanide and die together on purpose. I wondered if my babysitter wanted us kids to die just like them. He didn't offer us any Kool-Aid, but if he would have, I would've said "no thanks."

The total of two hours in the dark seemed pretty horrible and made me suppose that maybe school wasn't so bad after all. So when we all got freed from the basement to go home that night, I asked Mom if I could stay in my empty classroom after school instead of going back to that babysitter. Once she made a few phone calls, she said Toni and I should walk to the apartment of some neighbor lady named Darcey tomorrow after school. I had never met this woman, but the mention of her gave me a brief feeling of losing balance. Sometimes I get this feeling. And it always means I won't like what's coming.

Darcy had short yellow hair that spiked forward to set off her buck teeth. The way her teeth jutted out from under her lips made her look like she was always about to laugh and I would've liked that about her except I hated her from the second I saw her. There was such a weird tang in her indoor air—a mix of wet garbage, farts, and dog spit—that I had to hold my breath and use all the brainpower I had trying to craft a way to get permission to pop myself outside for a good clean inhale.

I think Darcy mistook babysitting to mean "just sitting" because that's all she did—in front of the TV. Toni and I kept ourselves entertained making drawings of Darcy's teeth on her own personal notepad to see how long she'd ignore us before she felt driven to check in on what we were doing.

Toni's drawings were by far the best, making me laugh so hard I got weak and I actually wet my pants, which for some reason made us both laugh even harder. I cackled myself to tears, thinking how funny it would be to strip off my wet clothes from the waist down and see if Darcy blinked. But then I had a better idea.

"Watch this," I said to Toni and grabbed the iron poker hanging near the fireplace, hooked my pants and underwear on its tip and dangled the proof of my spill between Darcy and the TV without saying a word. Toni exploded in amusement, impressed by my boldness.

"Just leave them," the sitter said, too engrossed by the steamy soap stars on the screen to get grossed out by my yellow underwear. My delirious giddiness flattened fast and grew into a temper surge I'd never felt before. I stood directly between her and the TV where she could not ignore me and raised the stakes by flinging the soggy clothes toward her face, due payback for leaving me bare bottomed. My garments stayed caught on the poker, though, only dropping to the floor by my feet at the tail end of my downswing.

Without any expression in the least, Darcy looked right through me, her eyes somehow still fixed on the television screen. She lit up a cigarette, inhaled slowly, and blew two cheekfulls of smoke out through her dry lips. Toni could see me lifting up the fireplace poker, getting ready to force Darcy to see me.

My sister stopped me before I could whack the heavy iron down on our babysitter's head. Toni took the poker, collected my clothes off the floor and pulled me away from Darcy into the next room.

"Just wrap your underwear inside your jeans and tuck them somewhere until Mom gets here," she said calmly, sensibly, taking charge once more as the most mature person in the house. I took her instruction, shoving the garments down inside the refrigerator fruit drawer where no one would see or smell them.

The whole thing felt wrong, walking back out into the living room to sit near Darcy with my naked fanny directly on her couch. Toni brought me a book she found on the shelf that I opened up to keep on my lap. Then she sat beside me real close so I didn't feel alone, looking off to the side of the room, biting her nails.

We knew all we could do was wait for help, for Mom to come pick us up. And when she did, you can bet that nobody was paid on that day.

Our last sitter Shamarra was the kind of sitter I'd always hoped for. She was round, dark-skinned and sweet like a giant chocolate cupcake.

At her house, kids would play in twos and threes in her vast half grassed, half paved front yard. They had toys in their hands, bike grease and chalk dust on their pants, and excitement in their eyes. I didn't need to join their games. I was happy just watching,

In truth I was a little scared to play, I guess. What if the minute I started to play, I would fall or stop breathing or do something really, really dumb? Everyone would laugh at me. Sometimes I'd try to play, but more often than not I'd end up having to go inside to the bathroom and feel the softness of the towels on my face just so I could get my breath back.

"You okay in there?" Shamarra would always notice when I was gone and she'd call to me with a soft voice through the bathroom door.

"Yes. Just a minute," I would say, scraping up enough liveliness to sound happy and normal. I would run the water like I was just washing up.

"Don't hurry, Jenna" she said. "Take your time."

So I would. I'd stand there tracing my fingers all around the borders of the small stone tiles covering the sink counter until I was in a sort of trance. It helped me feel better.

Shamarra had a cozy yellow chair where she would let me sit with her while she massaged Vaseline lotion on her feet. Her big warm body rocked back and forth while she rubbed her toes. The normal nature of it gave me a strange feeling of absolutely nothing being wrong.

"What were you like when you were a little girl?"

I asked Shamarra the simple question because I felt an opportunity for meaningful conversation opening.

"I imagine I was like every other girl who ever lived," she said with a bright face, clicking her plastic lotion bottle shut. "I wanted the world to be full of magic and rainbows and heroes on chariots." She laughed at her words.

"It's hard to have a world with magic when life keeps getting in the way to ruin it," I said, tracing the lines on my left open palm with my right finger, then looking up at her to see if she heard me.

She looked back at me surprised, like I just bit her tongue. But then her eyebrows relaxed right away. Her arms pulled me tightly to her plentiful body.

"Child," she said. "All little girls try to get by the best they know how. You'll be just fine. You'll see.

"Can you keep a secret?

She spoke again right away, maybe sensing "you'll be fine" wasn't convincing me.

"I can keep big secrets," I said, thinking of how I still haven't told anyone I sometimes wish I would fall over and die just to get away from life, how painful the urgency is of wanting to fix the world, and how dreadful living becomes when confusion lasts for years on end.

It turns out her secret was about me. She said I'm wise beyond my years.

"Honey, you're different, and that's the way the heavens intended you to be. You see things all the time that other kids don't even notice," she continued. "That's a very special thing."

Shamarra bet I could see what was going to happen before it happened. I nodded in agreement.

"I'd pay to get inside your head," she said and laughed deeply, shaking hers. "Then I could see clear past my little world."

Her words felt good from the inside. I had a proud feeling that someone good and kind would actually want to be inside my mixed up head. Maybe I had some good in me after all. For once I was glad to be a little girl. I was a girl just like Shamarra used to be—a girl who was getting by the best she knew how.

My Grandma's not in her room when I get home from sneaking out of Mrs. Root's class. She's out in the living room watering plants. So this is what she does when we're gone.

"What're you doin' home?" Grandma says.

The words practically stampede out of her mouth. She's probably been dying to say something to somebody all day.

"School let out early today," I lie.

"Oh," she says. And that's the end of it.

I thought I'd want to be outside after having escaped from Math class, but what I really want to do is close my bedroom door, lie in bed and watch the sunlight work with the wind and trees to make a stage show of dancing patterns on my wall.

My room feels different on a school day afternoon. Even the faces on my stuffed animals seem more lively than usual. Their smiles are bigger, I swear. Maybe it's because they'd planned to get together like this on my windowsill just to welcome me home.

I clasp my hands behind my head, satisfied to stare at a single point on the wall just above my sneakers. I let my mouth hang any way it wants. Just as the fluffiness of peace and contentment begins to ease my mind, I sense that the red monster is planning to wreck it.

Where is your Dad right now?

The throbbing monster appears as I feared, looking bloated, confident, and charged.

Maybe the grim reaper has come to get him.

I lunge at the happy animals on my windowsill, bunching them in my arms, a shield of smiling stuffing to scare away the bad thing in the room. Searching their faces for reassurance I hug them firmly. The monster shakes his fiery head and laughs at my attempt at self comfort.

Your play toys might help you little Jenna, but they won't help your Dad.

His scarlet words poke me in the chest like darts poisoned with sure defeat. All I can bear to do is lie still on my bed and clutch the sympathetic toys tight to my chest, trying to ease that dreadful piercing pain in my heart.

• • •

Instead of picking on me today, Mrs. Root has been telling funny jokes to the whole class about what she found last night in her cat's litter box. In some ways I want to stay in class to feel what it's like to laugh along with a roomful of people. But I just can't stop myself from seeing if I can walk out of school two days in a row. Plus I should call my Dad at work to see if he's ok.

So I'm back at Mrs. Root's desk telling another lie.

"I have a birthday party to go to," I say. "My Mom is picking me up in front of the school."

"Oh, that's nice Jenna." Mrs. Root's eyebrows rise high. "How about I wait for your Mom with you?"

"That's ok. I know my way out," I mumble nervously.

"Oh I insist. Rita McGee, you're in charge of the classroom," she announces. "I'll be back in a minute."

Mrs. Root takes hold of my hand, her thin gold bracelets rattling like handcuffs. She leads me hurriedly down the school's front steps, saying that we'd better not keep my mother waiting. My stomach instantly churns, then tightens with dread. I know there isn't going to be a car with my Mom in it anywhere around here. Still, I wait with Mrs. Root in front of the school with fake expectation.

I wring my hands, scratch my elbow and roll my shoulders to calm the nerve endings that are jumping around under my skin. It's as if my body is asking me why I'm waiting for a person to show up and steal me away when I know full well no one is ever going to come.

"Well that's strange..."

Mrs. Root says it in the same voice she uses when she's talking about me to the class.

"...your own mother forgot to show up to take you to a birthday party? That's not very nice of her. I guess we'll just have to go back to class and learn some Math."

My desk waits for me, empty like an open cage. I climb in and close the latch. And while I know I'm supposed to be adding up numbers, the only things I'm counting are the minutes until the bell rings.

Exactly one minute before the school day is over, Mrs. Root summons me for the dreaded inquisition.

"Jenna, come up here to my desk."

Sharp prickles barb my face like a thousand bee stings, flushing my cheeks and muffling the sound of my classmate's whisperings.

"Jenna, *who* is going to hold a birthday party in the middle of a school day?" Her voice booms. "How stupid do you think I am?" she demands, grabbing my jaw in an ice cold vice grip, squeezing so tight that my lips pucker like a guppy's.

"Well, how stupid?"

Does she really want me to answer that?

"Stupid enough?"

The roaring laughter of my classmates tells me that's the wrong answer. I get the feeling one furious teacher will be giving Mom a phone call after work.

The ringing phone makes me tremble. I wait nearby, trying to surmise what's coming. I pull at my right earlobe and look at the area of couch cushion that's exposed between my knees. Mom rubs her right temple in a counterclockwise circle as she hears the story through the receiver.

Maybe Mom won't get mad this time. She'll see it as an opportunity to ask something about me, like why I wanted to get out of school so badly. I listen and wait, raising my eyes only high enough to study the lower details of our living room. It's the first time I notice that our house doesn't look much emptier since Dad left. He didn't take much with him. In a lot of ways, it looks like nothing's changed around here at all. But it feels like everything has.

"Jenna," Mom says to me when she hangs up the phone. "Come and get your spanking."

8

Chalk Rainbows
Age 9, June 1980

Leaving a group of people behind gets you a ton of attention. The whole third grade class threw me a surprise party when they found out Mom was moving us all the way across town. You'd think people would hesitate to waste good cheer on you when they know you're leaving anyway. But it was all there; chips, punch, cookies, cheese puffs and bubble gum.

Right about the time the punch bowl was empty and everyone was supposed to sing "for she's a jolly good fellow" there was a loud heave and a splatter near the chalkboard. The sound called us all to turn our heads around and down at the same time.

You'd think that one pile of bright red throw up is probably the worst thing you could see at your going away party, but it's not the worst thing. The worst thing is when the sight of it sets off a chain reaction of puking that makes the whole room seem like a minefield, bombs of red barf blowing up all over.

Everyone was screaming, moving, shoving, and spitting up. Somehow I managed to keep my stomach even though the room smelled like a strong mix of rotten cherries and raw meat.

"Watch your step! Everybody stay calm."

I surprised myself taking charge like that. Everybody stopped screaming, waiting for me to say what to do next. Then when they realized I didn't know, they went back to screaming.

Soon afterward, the parents of my classmates had been phoned. A line of cars lingered outside the school, looking like some kind of funeral fleet. The cars were full of frantic Moms and Dads protectively swiping their kids from the school, looking over their shoulders with concern and suspicion.

I watched the cars angle out from the parental procession line one by one and into the moving street traffic, blending in with the mix of other drivers with their own lives, their own emergencies. I was the one who was supposed to be leaving my school, but it turned out my school had left me—demoted from 'jolly good fellow' to 'last classmate standing'.

Since my parents couldn't be reached, the teacher released me to walk home. The vacant hallway seemed soft and unthreatening suddenly. I could finally leave and never come back. School years are large accomplishments to put in our back pockets. The good feeling of that achievement was mixed with fear, however. It was uncomfortable being in between a teacher I hated and a new school I dreaded. Our upcoming move to Knightford Heights meant making another big switch—one that everyone seemed ready for but me.

A single voice and a song seemed to lift the afternoon shadows in the block of hallway where my old classroom had been. The music was magnetic, it drew me closer. It was a song my other grandparents Nanna and Poppy like to sing.

"I see sunflower fields, bouquets of pink blossoms, everything's roses, all tops and no bottoms, people got dreams and no one can stop 'em. It's a wonderful life. A wonderful life."

The crooning man danced all by himself, his mop stick flowing to and fro, dipping once and again into the lumpy cherry colored barf water in the bucket.

"Excuse me, sir?"

When I said it, I recognized his immaculate white shoes. And those kind eyes from the sidewalk.

"Ya can call me Frank," he said, like he was expecting me. Gently leaning his mop up against the chalkboard, he took a seat square on the nearest desktop. It was ok that he was facing me. He was still a safe distance across the room.

"I r'member you. Do ya r'member me?" Frank asked.

"From the sidewalk," I said. "You stopped to talk to me."

"Yessa did."

"You said you could help me. You said you understood. How do you know me?"

Those were the most words I'd ever spoken all at once to a stranger. I kept my distance, fearing the worst, but hoping for the best.

Frank took a deep bellied breath. He got up to set a bright yellow *Caution: Slippery When Wet* sign on the floor then returned to his seat atop the desk.

Pointing loosely up at the door to the hallway, he said "Now I ain't tryin' to be alone with no student in this classroom. People starta come up with some kinda scandal about the janitor messin' with school kids. But looka here, I'm thinkin' that the good Lord sent you to this room so I could tell ya what it is I understand about'cha.

"See, I was just like you when I was your age. Just miserable. Child, your mind is all full of worry. And that teacher you had, Mrs. Root, she didn't help but to make things worse for ya–didn't get to know how your brain works. But I'm gettin' off track."

I stepped backward, feeling awkward. I wanted him to shut up about me being miserable, but he kept talking.

"Let me put it to you straight, Jenna. All year long I would see you come and go from this school–see the whole story of your life in ya' eyes," he said. "And I can tell ya never had anyone tell you what the hell is going on inside your head. Not because they don' care to. Most people just don' see it. But I see it."

"See what?" This was the only other person I ever met who could see things about people without even getting to know them. It felt like on one hand I couldn't hide my feelings but on the other I didn't want to.

"You're what they call a deep thinker. You're a sensitive kid. It's a good thing. But people make you feel like you from anotha' planet sometimes, heh-heh, true or true?"

"Uh, true?" I thought that this was about the time to wake up from one of my weird dreams. I went over to the chalkboard so I could turn my back on the man but still listen. Tracing wide rainbows with pink chalk, I held my breath so I could hear the man clearly.

"When I seen you on the street I thought maybe I could help ya. All I was tryin' ta tell ya was don't let people make you think you got some kind of sickness or syndrome just because you think and feel diff'rent. Ain't nothing wrong with you. In fact, there's something right about kids like you. You care about things that matter down deep. You keep things in perspective and you got big hearts. Big hearts get broken terrible, but hey that's just the way God made you. Don't try to fight it."

I put down the chalk and started erasing my rainbows, still listening with interest, but acting like I had better things to do.

"Lord, I can tell you don't know the half of it yet. You're gonna have to figure this out for yo own self over time. I'd like to see you succeed, lil' girl. I'd like to see ya get a better chance than I had.

"This your movin' away party? Here, take ma phone number. If ya ever in a bind, use it and Uncle Frank can help getcha through."

Frank took a sheet of lined notebook paper and a red flair pen from the teacher's desk, wrote down seven neatly printed numbers and handed the sheet to me.

"And remember, you ain't alone. You gonna be fine. Lotsa people will help you if you ask. Ya see, ya can't just wish and hope for help. Ya gotta ask."

June 1980, playing outside during a weekend visit with my Dad and sister.

9

Life in the Heights
Age 9, Fall 1980

Mom's putting on lipstick in the car's rearview mirror, all the while backing over the grass and the curb to the left of the driveway.

It's our family's first full day living in Knightford Heights, a development on the outskirts of downtown Riverston–a place Mom's realtor calls "the suburbs." They call this "the heights" because it's just up the hill from the rusted, overgrown train tracks that the realtor says used to carry coal and steel across the state.

Our new neighborhood has rectangular houses and bright green lawns that have been plopped down along wide streets. The houses aren't all connected in rows like the one we've been living in. They're just connected in twos, split down the middle with two front doors, two front sidewalks, and two addresses.

I look at my Mom's lips getting color in the rear view mirror, then check out the back window to make sure we're not going to hit anything. Sometimes I feel better about my problems when I can predict other people's problems and fix them before they happen. I point out what might be wrong all the way to our new school because I need to distract myself from my fear of meeting new people.

I can feel the sweat start to sting my armpits when Mom turns off the car in the visitor's parking space in front of the school. My forehead tightens into that deep wrinkle my skin makes when I'm nervous. It's starting to stay that way–a worry line as my Mom calls it. She says it makes me look smart. Toni says it makes me look dumb.

"First thing's first. Hug your Mom goodbye and hug me hello."

The Knightford Elementary office lady greets us by opening out her arms to frame us up like a lovely picture. She acts like it's the most natural thing for a kid to hug a perfect stranger. Her dress is rose colored, very soft looking. I reach out to feel her skirt, finding it to be soft as a pussywillow pod in the first days of spring. That alone makes me willing to stay at our new school if Toni is.

The lady's hug leaves me smelling like perfume but also makes me let out a nervous fart.

"Let's go, superstars," she says, probably wanting to move on from the stinky air. She smiles a wide peachy-pink lipped smile to Mom, who takes the cue and hugs me and Toni goodbye.

"We'll take good care of them," the lady says.

I've heard that before. Adults make promises like that, knowing full well they aren't going to respond to your emergency if there is one. Like when the fire alarm goes off at your school and you don't get led out in perfectly formed lines like you're supposed to.

"Don't worry," the teachers say "it's just a false alarm" and so you just have to sit there at your desk and wait until the clanging stops, wondering if today's the day it's not a false alarm and you're all getting ready to burn.

"You'll be ok, Jenna."

My new fourth grade teacher Mr. Smarts doesn't turn his nose at me in disgust when I walk in the room. He doesn't even make me sit down beside my new classmates right away. Instead he asks me if I'm a good speller and hands me a fat piece of chalk and a list of words to write on the chalkboard. My heart pumps as fast as a dog panting.

Sliding the white chalk against the slate board instantly calms me. I like the idea of facing a wall instead of sitting with people who stare at you and expect you to know what to say to them. I chalk the vocabulary words on the board as slowly as I can so I will never have to sit at my desk in the middle of huge a stack of strangers.

I focus on the blackboard, imagining it to be the night sky, daydreaming of the hours I'll soon spend looking out my window after dark tonight. That's my favorite time of day, when everybody else is sleeping. That's when things get real again. The stars come to life. The world outside sounds less like noise and more like nature. Sounds of life outside my bedroom window cover me with a blanket of calm, sending me into a deep peaceful sleep.

As I carve out each white letter, I dream up a set of lies that I might tell my new teacher if I feel the urgency to get out of class immediately. I am only ten blocks from home, so if I get plagued by people at school maybe I can leave out of here–heading straight for the woods behind my house to spend the day.

I can already hear the whistles and shrieks of the afternoon birds calling and the shhhhh of tree branches blowing in the breeze. I might bury my body in a pile of dry leaves and lie there, smelling the clean rot under the brightness of the sun. Or I could just relax against bulging tree roots beneath their strong arms then move on to snapping sticks and studying stones, smelling flowers and feeling fuzzy moss with my toes in the wettest places of the woods until school officially lets out.

Mr. Smarts interrupts my daydream with words from a book called "A Stitch in Time." He's pointing me to an empty desk as he reads. I dust off my hands and take a seat in my new chair. Mr. Smarts' story instantly turns my imagination on red hot like the electric coils on Mom's stovetop burner. I forget that I ever wanted to leave this class. The story gives me the feeling I used to get when coloring my favorite coloring book, letting the waxy shades stretch way outside the lines.

Colors, places and creatures lift up out of this story, giving me a herd of ideas that I want to lasso and fix fast to a tale of my own making. And an hour after Mr. Smarts closes today's chapter of "A Stitch in Time" I get my chance.

My first Knightford Elementary School English class assignment is to write an essay answering the basic question; "Where do you want to go?"

I practice the answer to that question in my head every second I get a chance, so I don't understand why we're taken to the library and taught how to use Encyclopedia Britannica to find the answer. Why would people need to look for an answer to where they want to go in a book that somebody else wrote?

While everyone's looking up facts on Paris and New Orleans and Jamaica, I stay in my seat, penciling dark spirals of cursive across and down my paper, spreading shiny gray graphite on the pinky side of my right hand.

I take the assignment home after school and spend two more hours writing in my room. It's hard trying to dream up the words to explain where I want to go, though. It has to be a place that's best for everyone.

I finally create a picture of a new world in words–a place where you stay asleep always, where your dreams are in full color cartoons. I write that you can do anything in this place–you can "be anybody, any race, any animal, have any face."

Just the thought of living there makes me laugh with a cheerfulness I didn't know I had. This essay is more like the real me than anything I've ever put on paper so far. I read my own personal creation nine times, then ten more times later after dinner.

• • •

"What does plah-gear-ized mean?" Looking way up to Mr. Smarts from my low library chair, I wonder how I appear to him from where he's standing.

"Jenna, I gave you an 'F' because you copied your essay from somewhere else. I'm surprised at you," he says, closing the abandoned encyclopedia at the far end of my table for effect. "You have to do your own work if you want to get ahead. There's no way around it."

Mr. Smarts squats down to below my eye level. "What I want to know is where you copied it from," he says. "You've got until the bell rings to tell me. Otherwise, you're going to the principal's office."

I pull the cuffs of my sleeves down overtop of my hands to make them disappear. Kicking at the legs of the chair in front of me a few times, I wait for Mr. Smarts to see through me. I can usually tell when people are lying and when they are telling the truth. I'm sure he'll be able to tell, too, if he looks hard enough.

Fully anticipating his apology I kill time until the bell rings by adding a line to the bad grade on top of my essay, changing the F into a squarish looking A. Once I've filled the top of my paper with plus signs around the new A, the bell sounds.

"Jenna. Office. Now," Mr. Smarts says.

The principal's office is in the sunny part of the school—the place where they keep trophies and post banners that say encouraging things, like "each student is an original masterpiece."

The school principal walks toward me saying, "Oh look, there's Jenna. Miss Jenna, your art teacher and I were just talking about you."

I'm mesmerized by how her long navy polka dotted dress swings back and forth from where it's cinched at the waist. Her high heels have glittery stones near the toes which accent the shimmering diamond ring and wedding band she wears together on her left hand.

"Mr. Smarts made me come here because he says I copied on my writing project. He gave me an F, but I didn't cheat, I *swear*." I hold my hands palms up in front of me when I say it, with my elbows bent, like I'm waiting for two handfuls of mercy.

"Let me see what you wrote," she says. My face flushes, knowing she's going to see that I turned the F into an A plus. I pull the folded pockmarked paper out of the front of my English book and open it. The cursive is already fading into silver smears.

As the principal reads, I look down at my feet, comparing the scuff marks on my shoes with those on the floor, hoping my words are no longer readable. The quiet stretches on too long, but I don't want to look up to the principal's eyes just in case they will give away what she thinks of my words. Instead, I search the lobby for hidden imperfections and easily find a flaw in a nearby baseboard. Rocking back and forth nervously from toes to heels, I speculate on how long the baseboard blemish has been left that way.

"I believe you, Jenna," The principal finally says. "You seem like you might be able to create a good story. I'll talk to Mr. Smarts about bringing up your grade." She hands my paper back to me.

"You've got some art talent, too, so your art teacher says. Mrs. Hoskins was just by our office and she says you showed great aptitude in her class yesterday. My guess is she wants you to be in the school's Art Club. Do you know what the Art Club does?"

She doesn't wait for me to answer, thank God.

"It makes the school look more colorful—more alive."

Ever since Mom and Dad divorced and the red monster said Dad was going to die, I stopped putting color on blank paper. I quit filling it with all my ideas that came from who knows where. Instead, I put the colors away because they didn't seem to make a pretty picture no matter how hard I tried. But today, the words "more alive" made the highest hair on my head stand up. So that settles that. I'm going to make art again.

"If your art talent is half as good as your essay, we're in for a good looking school," my new principal adds, walking off, attending to other school business.

I pretend to be pausing to fold my assignment back into my book, but I'm really staying out of class for this extra minute to size up the trophies in the glass case in front of me.

Some have gold plates at the bottom that say "high achievement" with a student's name below. Some awards are for my actual school. I didn't know a whole school could win a trophy. If my school can win a trophy, and I am part of this school, then maybe I can be good enough to have an award in a glass case someday, too.

Tap, tap, tap. I drum on the glass with my index finger with thought producing percussion. Every possibility is right there inside the display in gold plated form. The case is dazzling. It's giving me ideas. I wonder if I won an award, what it might be for. What can I be best at? All this time I've been trying to be good enough to get by, but what if I were better or best?

Mr. Smarts is waiting for me outside the door of our classroom with a sheet of blank paper.

"Go across the hall to the library and write me a few paragraphs about your favorite subject," he says. "If it's really good, I'll change your F to an A. You've got fifteen minutes."

Normally having a time limit on anything makes me queasy and weak in my bones because it's hard to make things come out perfect if you're distracted by a ticking second hand. But this assignment won't be hard. All I need to do is write about what my inside voice blabs on about all day while the outside of me is sitting there with my mouth shut as if I don't have a thought in the world.

I snatch the paper, rush past the librarian, and find a table in the emptiest corner of the library. Thankfully, no classes are here to bother me with chitter chatter. I am so excited by the chance to redeem myself that I push my pencil too hard into the paper.

Click. My pencil point snaps in a splintery mess of lead and wood.

I trip on the leg of my table on the way to the sharpener, scratching my arm with the frayed wood tip in my haste. The clock ticking, I lunge at the handle, speedily rotating it into the sharpening tool. Checking and blowing the tip a few times, I grind out the perfect point.

"Jenna?" The librarian notices my lone presence in her territory. "Did your teacher give you permission to come here?"

"Go ask him." I point towards my classroom with my left hand without looking up, rushing back to my table.

"Jenna, don't be smart."

"Sorry. I have an essay and my time is going fast," I say, blocking her out with a hunched posture that's meant to tell her to keep away. My elbows point out east to west to protect and defend my chance for redemption.

The librarian gets distracted by some teachers that wander in to quietly talk grade-level logic.

I tune them all out and write as fast as I can. The words are hardly readable, but I get them on paper:

People say I think too much, that touching and rushing shouldn't be so overwhelming but I'm telling it from my skin because it's the one I happen to be wearing. It's scary to be so aware of how people aren't caring for kids on the street, animals in need, tumbling trees and polluted streams. Sometimes I wonder if life's a dream that it's a river I'm swimming, without any oars in a boat that is tipping. I'm looking and waiting for the answer to be stated, I'm hating just waiting for some help that's not coming. It makes me wonder if there's something I'm supposed to be doing besides waking and sleeping and getting through nothing. My stomach is rumbling because the clock's ticking, so I'd better finish this essay. I can see the teacher's coming.

Mr. Smarts gave me an A. The essay was entered into a contest that won, so I got to read it in front of the school.

10

Unbreakable
Age 10, Spring 1981

Four students are assigned the special Art Club project of painting murals on a row of windows in the school hallway. We'll be allowed to paint an hour after school for a whole week. As luck would have it, three to four o'clock just happens to be the time of day when the afternoon sun shines through those very windows and onto our enthused faces.

"You can paint any scene you want."

Mrs. Hoskins squirts globs of tempera paint onto our plastic palettes. I dab my brush in the color instantly, knowing exactly how I want the people to be greeted. With bold brushstrokes I fill the glass canvas with chunky layers of greens, blues and oranges plus a dot here and there of red. My square of glass is turning into a layered nature scene, a springtime landscape that will make people think of fresh starts and new beginnings.

The painted glass returns a reflected view of my own eyes when a cloud passes over the sun. I'm not searching my reflection for what's missing this time. Every part of me is where it's supposed to be.

When it comes time to clean up, Mrs. Hoskins tells us to wash the paint down the drain.

"But it'll make the water dirty," I tell her. "And paint isn't good to drink." I take her out to the water fountain and show her where the water comes back out after it's gone down the drain.

"We can't make more water," I explain. "It just keeps going round and round again."

"That's true, Jenna, but the water gets cleaned first."

"But they can't clean paint out of water."

"Um."

Mrs. Hoskins said I should talk to my science teacher to make sure the class knows what happens to the water in our city. I did what she said so everybody in my class would have to think about the systems we depend on for life.

For our second Art Club project, we built one giant paper maché statue of E.T. We're rolling it out at tonight's spring chorus concert. Mrs. Hoskins rigged up a light bulb inside his body and taped red cellophane paper over a small open spot on the lefthand side of his chest. She said she'll switch the light bulb on during my grade's special song *Heartlight* because it will really bring the lyrics to life.

When it comes time for my class to perform our rehearsed songs at the spring concert, I feel part of something big. Onstage, five levels of grade schoolers on risers crunch in tight from beside, above and below. A band of lights shine toward us, then dim dramatically, signaling to us it's time for us to sing *Heartlight*.

Just as Mrs. Hoskins planned, our sculpture's light bulb clicks on, making E.T.'s chest glow red like a stop light. Parents gasp with pleasure at the alien's heart, making me smile so big I can hardly bring my lips together to belt out the words.

Of all the forty-three kids singing this song, there's no doubt I'm the proudest. It makes me feel so incredibly hopeful knowing my parents are watching me sing. Even though they're sitting on separate sides of the auditorium, I believe that their hearts are starting to burn warm with hope, too. Soon I'll be standing once again inside one complete and unbreakable family circle.

After the event, I proudly steer my Mom, Dad and Toni through the halls of my school, radiating a new air of confidence. *Jenna* is printed in big letters on my art and essays taped up alongside all the other students' work. With each portrait or poem of mine that my parents observe, I have a shot at witnessing their reactions of unhampered joy. This is the test to see if something of my creation can make some instant miracle happen in their hearts.

It *is* possible. After all, my art helped me like my own reflection. And my essay made my teacher see truthfulness. If words and paint can do that, then surely they can cause anything to come about, even something as impossible as my parents falling in love again.

"I thought your Dad was dead?"

A girl named Diane interrupts my daydream just as my parents are reading my finest essay. Diane's my best friend. Actually, she's my only friend. She's the only one I've told that my Dad's going to die.

"Jenna, *who's* that tall guy?" Diane won't let up.

"It's my Dad, dummy," I say pulling her aside. I wish she'd go away long enough to let my parents ponder my fantastic writing. They need some uninterrupted time to remember how they made beautiful talented children together, children who could really be champions if given half the chance.

"Not dead, then?" she snorts. I look up at my Mom and Dad to make sure they didn't just hear Diane's question.

"Not yet, stupid," I whisper, rolling my eyes like she's the dumbest person alive. "I told you it's *going* to happen any day now."

• • •

Diane's actually far from being the dumbest person alive. She's truly the best. This tall, skinny, goofy girl trips on purpose and fake picks her nose just to make me laugh. She invents gadgets out of paperclips during homeroom and writes me funny notes with cartoon drawings of our teachers.

Knowing I'm supposed to be seriously studying is half of what makes her notes so funny, the other half of course being sheer comedy. Diane's notes have gotten me sent to the principal's office for a second, third and fourth time in the span of just one month. Luckily, Diane is home sick today so I'm back to being my old shy and quiet self.

"Jenna, go to the principal's office right away," Mr. Smarts sneaks up right behind me during study time and for once he's caught me right in the middle of actually studying.

"But I wasn't even doing anything this time!"

"Oh you're not in trouble Jenna," Mr. Smarts says shaking his head, stooping down to squat level. He's speaking in a loud whisper, the hushed tone that's way louder than talking because it's so obvious you're whispering that everyone listens.

"Your Mom just called the school. She said there's a family emergency."

"Did my Dad die?" I utter in a grave murmur, clasping my hands together and squeezing tight. Today could be the day.

Mr. Smarts stacks up my books and hands them to me as he scoots me out the classroom door.

"Just go get your emergency release slip from the office. Your Mom is coming to get you right away."

With my pink slip in hand and a principal's escort out of my school, I realize I'm finally getting the emergency escape from class I've wanted for so long. But now I'm not so sure I want it.

From where I stand I can see Mom's rusted white Volare flying up the hill towards my school, barreling into the parking lot. Mom hits the gas instead of the brake again, making Toni's springy curls fly back then whip forward as the engine roars. The car lurches toward the curb where I stand, coming to a sudden stop at my toes.

The principal gets a distracted nod from my Mom who's already climbing into the back seat to sit with my sister. Mom flings the door open and pats the empty seat beside her, inviting me to sit down with the same voice she used the day she told us she and Dad were getting that crappy divorce.

"Jenna, be a good girl and get in the car." The look on her face is like I bet she looked like when she was a kid my age, still emotional.

I don't want to get in.

"Jenna, let's go, this is serious."

My body fits in snug once the door is closed. Stiff school books crest hard and heavy on my bony knees. On the other side of Mom, Toni squirms and twirls her strawberry curls with inky fingers. I consider how the brown vinyl car seat seams could have been sewn together a bit straighter.

Mom gets right to the news at hand—that it wasn't Dad who died after all. It was his brother Tom.

"Oh my gosh it's Tom?"

My relief for my Dad being fine is a short lived coup. Uncle Tom is one of my Dad's youngest brothers, the one in the family who I feel the most comfortable around.

Tom's shy like me, but still holds up his part of the conversation. He always has something original to say in a lively, smiling way. And when he isn't busy studying textbooks for tests, he's reading his favorite novels or watching the treetops from the windows of Nanna's house. I remember best the one time I went to join him gazing outside and we sat happily in silence together.

"How'd he die?" Toni sobs, throwing two pink hands onto her freckled cheeks. The webs between Toni's fingers catch strands of tears before they can reach her chin.

"Tom was poisoned by turning on the car in the garage. The smoke from the exhaust killed him but he didn't feel any pain. It's like he just went to sleep forever." Wet pathways form over Toni's hands and weave toward her wrists.

"Why?" I ask. Mom looks very serious, slightly worried, maybe even scared, even though the worst has already come to pass. There's no use in being afraid now, is there?

"He left a note saying he thought nobody loved him."

"But Uncle Tom was a grown up."

I don't know why I say this. I guess because you'd think that when you get to be as old as eighteen and as smart as a high school graduate, you finally have it all figured out.

Toni and I always looked forward to being eighteen for that very reason. Age eighteen is when people can tell you what to do, but you don't have to listen anymore. It's a time when you feel on top of the world because you're finally old enough to make decisions for your own life.

But I guess if you carry all your feelings around as heavy as a two ton truck like Uncle Tom must have, you don't care that you're old enough to make your own plans and start your new life. You just want to start that car in the garage, close your eyes, and float up to heaven.

I hope with all my heart that when Tom was sitting in the parked car looking through his tears past that clouding windshield, he started to see very clearly in front of him a great unknown place just outside this Earth, a more kind and loving place, where all the love in the world is there for the taking.

I keep my eyes closed and make a wish for myself— that I won't ever try to go to heaven like Tom did because heaven will come to me on Earth instead, appearing smack dab in front of me any day now.

I open my eyes to look at my Mom, remembering what the janitor said to me that day in my old classroom;

"Ya can't just wish and hope for help," he said. "Ya gotta ask."

"Mom?" I say.

"What, hon?"

"How do you…"

"How do you…what?"

Mom reaches for the back seat car door handle. She's headed to the driver's seat so she can get us home. I hold onto my question the second I realize my parents aren't the ones to answer this question. After all, if my Mom or Dad knew anything about bringing heaven down to Earth they would have done it by now. I roll down my car window to feel the outdoor air cool my face, drumming up a different question altogether.

"How do you dress for a funeral?"

11

Nonsense and Sensitivity
Days Later

When I get up close to Tom's coffin, there's this hollow sensation in my gut that tells me he's not anywhere near where I'm standing. It's as if my uncle has been replaced by one of those fake rubber people you see around Halloween. Toni told me that cousin Felicia said she heard a person weighs seven pounds lighter just after they die and nobody knows why. When she said it the hair on my arms stood on end like it knew something I didn't.

I don't see any point to me being here if he's not. But I still bow my head just like everybody else has done, folding my hands solemnly. Remembering things about Tom brings him back to the room, like the way his gemlike green eyes tended to be focused down and away and how you could still feel that he was one hundred percent there with you.

I peek at his face covertly to see if his eyes give a hint of where he is today. But the secrets behind those jeweled pupils are hidden under heavy lids. Wait. I should be saying a prayer or something. But if God knows anything it's that I have no idea how to pray. I retreat softly from the altar and walk the worn red carpet back to my family's pew. Everyone's whispering about how real they think Tom looked in his casket. It bothers me that they're telling lies inside a church.

Ya gotta ask for help.

That voice of Frank's resounds from somewhere suddenly, making me gasp in surprise, like my old school janitor has got to be standing in the pew right behind me.

Nobody's back there though but my cousins and Aunt Barbara. They're looking down at their open hymnals, ready to sing the first song of eulogy.

Seated but uneasy, I kick my heels against the wooden underside of my pew, wondering why Frank's voice is in my head telling me to ask for help. Can't he see I'm doing fine–that I don't need any help? At school I'm learning to sing, do art and I've made a good friend too.

It's as simple as this: When the time comes that my life starts to get really, really bad again I *will* call Frank and ask him for help.

I will. I promise.

But I just don't need help right now.

What's happenin' right now? Frank's unmistakable voice once again rattles inside my head.

Happening now? I stall to consider the thought. With a final blast the organ marks the end of the hymn, leaving me a severe space of dead silence to mull it over.

A funeral. Now a funeral is happening, I admit, repeating the notion to let the reality of it sink in. *Now is a funeral, now is a funeral.* I let the words bend and fold in my mind while my Dad and his brothers close and seal Uncle Tom's casket.

Sound pretta bad ta me. Frank makes his point known in a whisper. He thinks my life is a mess. I know it.

Shut up. It's not bad.

I wish that voice of his would let up. I fix my mind on playing a word game. Playing with new ideas always helps me hush the bothersome echo of disappointment running marathons through my brain.

If now is a funeral, then what's a funeral? I think to myself, launching my private word game. *What's a funeral, what's a funeral?* I tap my finger on my legs to the rhythm of the words, looking around the church, feeling guilty for being so lost in thought. I feel bound to the question.

What is a funeral?

An ending?

Everyone's turning the page of their programs. I follow suit, pretending to be following along. The words *A Turning Point* crest the top of the second page. We're asked to read the printed poem out loud.

> Let our great loss remind us
> that though life is not always kind to us,
> it is our faith that defines us.
> And so we ask, and we believe, that we are redeemed
> and thus paradise and glory now finds us.

A funeral is not necessarily an ending, but a turning point, a time for renewed conviction. If that's all true then maybe Tom didn't leave our family with nothing but a hopeless note after all. A grander message may have been made—the boldest suggestion to take urgent action to show people love right now. As far as Tom was concerned, I guess he felt love couldn't wait one more minute. If his spirit were here at this funeral today, I'd bet it would say "you'd better hurry up and decide if you're going to love or not, because some people haven't got a whole lifetime to wait."

After the service, everybody rises and bends toward the pews in shaky synchronicity, stooping intermittently like pressed piano keys to pick up hats, programs, and pocketbooks. I stay about three feet behind my sister, trusting her to lead me through the thick maze of mourners straight to the reception hall. At the kid's table Toni fishes me out a napkin and passes me a plate and a drink so that I'm all set up.

"Franks n' beans?" There's a lady in pearls and too much perfume passing out bowls of hot food to the kids.

"Is Frank here?" I ask her, thinking that maybe I was hearing his voice after all. All the kids laugh, like I tried to be funny. I go along with it, laughing, too.

"Franks are hot dogs," Toni whispers, then holds out her hands and says, "Give me some, please."

The fragrant frank and beans lady dishes out a bowl to my sister, then waits for me, holding her pot and ladle, ready to scoop.

"Make a decision, honey," she says. "We haven't got a whole lifetime."

12

Butterflies and Clothespins
Age 10, Summer 1981

Dad's late again. Sometimes Mom says his tardiness has nothing to do with us. "It's just a symptom involving the clock and his off base relationship with it," she's said. But at other times she's hinted that it's our fault he's late—because we're bad kids.

I know she doesn't mean it. It's just that every so often her temper just charges ahead of her heart. And stopping the words that come out is like trying to halt a train with nothing but a flimsy piece of hanger wire.

I never look at the clock when I'm waiting for my Dad. Instead I keep my brain busy doing other things. Like today I'm inspecting my third and fourth grade class pictures that are overtly displayed on the living room wall. Comparing the differences in my face between those two years is a good way to measure how I'm doing in life.

Side by side, the pictures of me don't look that much different from each other. In both pictures, I have a crooked hair part, a crooked collar, and crooked teeth.

I distinctly remember last year's picture day because our class photographer was a clown. He performed tricks before he took our photos, honking a horn when he handed us each our free black plastic comb. I thought the comb was just our door prize for watching his clown show. It didn't even occur to me to actually *use* the comb on my head.

But so what if my hair wasn't combed straight for my school snapshots? I still feel pretty good about myself because I did the best I could to be the real me. Deep down that's all that really matters, anyway. And I'm confident that there's a good part in every person that will see that. They won't focus on the little things that are wrong with me. Instead they'll zoom right in on the fact that I'm somebody special. And they will love me just exactly as I am.

Dad's car appears in our driveway later than ever, but he emerges full of so much warmth that it makes the wait worthwhile. Dad's hug puts me in higher spirits than anyone on Woodwind Street. I dive in the car and watch with delight the familiar scenery passing behind us as we disappear from the neighborhood, heading across the river and up into the mountains.

Since about two weeks before school let out, I've been looking forward to hanging freshly washed clothes on the line outside to dry with Nanna. It makes the whole yard smell of soap and clean laundry, fresh fabric that seems to bring white butterflies dancing around. I can picture the white sheets and green towels, each corner delicately snapped up with wooden clothespins.

At first I didn't think it was worth taking the time to hang your wash and pull it back down again. I changed my mind when I first smelled the outdoors on the indoor sheets and towels as I slept.

Nanna is almost as tall as Poppy when she's in one inch heels. Her eyes are big and round with eyelids that sit slightly low, making her look both wise and tired. She rubs her face and plops her hands down to smooth out the tablecloth repeatedly while she tells stories at the table. She is so easy with her words, so interesting that I just follow what she says. Everybody does.

Poppy is a natural at living, too. He's comfortable and sweet, sitting back with his glasses reading and humming, good and calm like a warm pond. He laughs with Nanna even after forty years together. Sometimes for fun she sits on his lap and let's him tumble her off-center for an extra kick of joy.

When I'm at Nanna and Poppy's, I don't have to figure things out for myself like where I want to go, how I'm going to find a way to get there, and what I'm going to have to eat along the way. All I need to do is show up and enjoy myself. The thought of it helps me let go and get lost in the soft looking forests and gurgling cold water creeks along the roadside, life itself rushing by my car window in a calming green and blue streak.

Dad puts extra pressure on the gas pedal when we start to pass street names like Cemetery and Church. That tells me we're about to arrive at Nanna's house on the hill, a lone brick building in the countryside that looks as stable as a fort from its driveway.

My Dad's childhood home had to be large enough to raise ten children. Because there were so many kids, Nanna and Poppy kept systems in place so everyone had a clear direction to follow. That's the kind of environment that works for me, where I know what the rules are so I don't have to worry about doing the wrong thing.

The three of us get out of the car to scale the stairs upward. I easily master the tall brick steps that used to trip me up when I was smaller. Nanna and Poppy's front balcony is the size of a stage. It doesn't matter that it's now summertime. This porch always reminds me of winter, the annual holiday sendoff specifically. It's my grandparent's tradition to stand and shiver outside, waving us down the frozen road with good wishes and great piles of gifts on our laps.

Nanna's house brightens up with voices from the kitchen when we come in. Aunts and Uncles call for us to get our hugs and kisses. I guess with Uncle Tom gone we're doing better to fill the house with as much love as possible.

My favorite heaven is going for a walk behind Nanna's house and under a shelter of trees to get to a garden so full and tall you can't see the end of it no matter which end you stand on. Poppy's garden is the reason we have so many vegetables at Nanna's meals. The brimming bowls of buttery corn, carrots and peas are full of a thick layered true vegetable flavor so unlike the dried up vegetable snacks that the Harrie County school nutrition ladies try to pass off on us for one week every year.

But none of these things are even the best thing about visiting Nanna's house. The best thing is that there's absolutely no loud TV or music around to take the focus away from the visit itself. Simple conversation is the center of the visit—clever wit and lively chatter. For hours and hours it's nonstop talk in the kitchen, only ending when everybody is about to burst from snacks and collapse from drinks and hooting laughter.

Because Nanna and Poppy believe in giving kids a good upbringing, they spend some time each day of our visit teaching my sister and me things like the proper way to make a bed, how to set the table, how to iron and fold sheets, and how to act at a Catholic church.

But they don't make us do anything we don't want to. They don't say "here's how to iron sheets" and then leave us with a pile of sheets to iron. They just show us how to do things in case we want to know. They do all the actual work themselves. Maybe because they know how hard we work at home, that this is our three weeks to just let loose and play like kids should.

Downstairs is the door to the garage where Uncle Tom died. I always feel strange going near it, wondering how you keep on living in a house where that reminder is always there to haunt you. I snap out of the thought when Poppy calls me upstairs, offering to pay me a nickel for every fly I can swat on the back porch. I trip up the carpeted steps, excited for the challenge.

Half an hour of swatting passes like half a second because I am one hundred percent happy in my bare feet and shorts and tank top standing around the sunny picnic table on the back porch, trying to see the most flies I can kill in one single whack, which ends up being three.

By the end, I count 39 of them killed, big black bodies lying all over the porch with their spindly legs always facing up. I find Poppy in the cool kitchen flopping cards down three by three on the table in front of rows of cards feathered out to look like a peacock's tail. I grab a chair at the table, hoping soon to be sipping a cold drink like the one he's got.

"I killed thirty-nine flies, Poppy."

"Well, that's great" He plops down his cards and smiles at me, smacking the flats of his hands on his knees for affect and then opening his arms out to welcome a hug. "C'mere you."

When he hugs me, all I can think about is how he actually believes that when I say I killed 39, I mean 39. He doesn't accuse me of lying and refuse to give me money. He doesn't walk out onto the porch and say, there aren't thirty-nine dead flies here. No, Poppy just hugs me and reaches for his wallet and hands me two dollars.

That's just about the time Nanna walks in the room with a smart dress on, her hair all tied up fancy for no other reason than to look pretty.

"What would you like to eat?" She asks in a rhythmic sing song way, already unloading the refrigerator, unwrapping trays of pickles and cheese and cold salads. Setting out boxes of Ritz crackers and Triscuits. I ask for an Oscar Meyer bologna, lettuce and mayonnaise sandwich with Fritos. Nanna makes my plate up just the way they look in the Fritos commercials.

The soft white bread forms a mass on the roof of my mouth, making me have to suck the food off with my tongue. The combination of flavor tastes so good I don't want to swallow. Making sure I've savored every last ounce of flavor in the sandwich, I wash it down with several swigs of milk, thinking about how right I was about how simple life can be.

I put my empty milk glass down, the last remnants of the white wash sliding down the insides, reflecting funny images of my sister, my Nanna, and my Poppy. Their milk glass faces look stretched wide like silly putty, chewing the good food on their plates, too.

Toni doesn't talk all the way through meals at Nanna and Poppy's like she does at home, so she and I finish our sandwiches at the same time. Together we yell,

"Thanks for lunch!" and run in a coordinated way out the kitchen door to the top of the steep grass bank in the back yard.

We roll down the hill like hotdogs, laughing enough to inhale specs of dirt and a blade or two of cut grass, tumbling enough to stain our elbows and knees and make our bottoms green. A few more hill rolls leave us covered with sticky pine sap.

I dare Toni to taste the sap to see if it's any good. I think it might be because maple syrup comes from trees and it's delicious. Toni licks the sappy patch on the back of her arm but instantly spits it out with disgust. So I don't try it myself. I just laugh at her sourpuss face.

The sap-dropping is coming from a huge tree sitting just above the grass bank. Its bark has yellowish icicles dangling all over it, summer icicles, soft warm ones that bend and pull like taffy.

Crack. I pull off a piece of bark just because it looks like it breaks off so easily.

Crack. Crack. Toni breaks off two more. It's just too tempting.

"The bark is loose on this tree because people once used it as a tool to study its icicles," I instruct Toni, making up the facts as I go. I'm always teaching her things about science and nature.

Scraping and pulling at the soft gel now, Toni and I compete to see who can make the sap stretch into the longest string without it breaking. While we play, shiny beetles and armored ants climb up and down the bark, carrying on with work, always on task. They're busy as the bees that buzz on and around the honeysuckle growing at the base of this pine.

We stop our game to study the insects whose entire world is this one massive tree, our small bare feet planted at it's base, twenty pale toes fixed firm in the dirt amidst a scatter of fallen pine cones.

Further away from the house now, we try to catch field crickets as they chirp and pop as high as our burr covered shorts. I study the winged varmints in flight, their shelled, twiggy body parts rasping up through the air and back down into the early summer brush.

This is how I wish we'd learn about subjects at school—by looking and listening, guessing and pondering, gathering all kinds of ideas and pictures in our minds all at once, then exploring them, by asking, testing, suggesting, finding and figuring.

After our supper of sliced ham, green peas, buttered carrots and applesauce, Nanna runs my bath first because I'm the youngest.

Lathering up a wash cloth to scrub off my dusty legs and sappy elbows, I accidentally turn my washcloth brown. My bath water is no better. A dark layer of dirt and skin skims the top of the tub making me feel gross.

I get the thought of my life being like that, like a person trying to get clean in dirty water. But I still go under to wash my hair and somehow the grimy water cleans me, making me feel a hundred times lighter. When the water drains I watch all my muck go down with it and I rinse the tub so I don't leave any sign of it behind.

My toes spread wide on the fluffy bath mat, leaving flat wet footprints like the first astronauts left on the moon.

I feel like I've landed. The towel Nanna left for me is purple and soft like the lavender flowers she and Poppy grow in the side yard. I squeeze the towel over my head, then wrap the damp cotton around me to change for bed in the guest bedroom.

Toni's still looking mighty dirty, especially sitting next to two bright white paper shirt boxes.

"I already opened them both," Toni says, putting her book down to go run her own bath. "They're presents from Nanna."

I lift the box tops, searching under folds of white tissue paper for the unexpected gift, a brand new nightie!

While Toni bathes, I decide that damp flowery hair is best air dried by parading around our guest room in brand new bedclothes. My sister soon joins me and we strut like soapy smelling queens modeling our new silky soft peach colored summer nightgowns. Our pageant wins the prize for the most elegant versions of sisters you've ever seen.

Nanna's come in our room now to gather our dirty clothes for washing, and Toni and I continue our proud procession behind her, following her lead out through the living room and into the kitchen.

Acting respectful in the kitchen like Nanna's taught us, we sit tight waiting for bowls of ice cream to have as a bedtime snack. I shoot a long thick tube of syrup on top of my bowl of plain vanilla ice cream to turn it into a rich dark puddle of frozen chocolate. It takes me half an hour to finish the treat because every spoonful of good food has to be slowly relished.

Licking off my brown, sticky lips, I finally bring my empty dish up to the double sink where Nanna's been working so intently on scrubbing up dishes.

When she moves aside to let me put my bowl in the sink I can see it's not dishes she's been working on after all. She's scrubbing stains from Toni's and my clothes. It's the first time I've really taken a good look at all the dirty blotches. I'm embarrassed that I didn't know enough to scrub them myself.

But I don't show my embarrassment. I just set my bowl down and walk away like I didn't see a thing.

13

Heaven as a Haven
One Year Later, Age 11, June 1982

Having an x-ray view on the world means you pick up on things pretty easily. It lets you plan ahead for what's coming. And you can naturally sense what people feel and what kind of help they need.

Maybe Mom has this sense, too. Perhaps it's why this morning I woke up to find a note on my dresser that said "Church on Sunday."

"I've been saying for years that I wanted to get you girls going to church," Mom said with pride when she saw me reading the note.

I didn't know we were religious, but after this past year, I'll try just about anything to get a little hope in my heart.

This past year was about getting tough, fighting the cause of some weaker people, getting into some harmless scraps for the underdog. Winning each battle was a cinch, maybe because I felt so sure it was right. The presence of something powerful was behind me every time the bad guy took the fall.

Offering protection to all my feeble, fatigued, deficient, or otherwise delicate classmates kept me from worrying about them. It also bolstered my confidence. As their problems got solved, I would feel entitled to focus on my own predicaments. As the year passed, however, my misfortunes never won the precedence I expected to give them.

When Sunday arrives Mom's up especially early, ready to run out the door for the nine o'clock worship service.

"Hurry up we're leaving now!"

"But it's only eight a.m." I say.

"Get your shoes on. We're late," Mom yells, tossing me my shoes, knowing full well it's impossible to catch two shoes at once.

Toni's blow dryer sounds full blast from the bathroom, which conveniently drowns out Mom's latest mandate. But that hot air reprieve only works for so long. When the whirring stops, Mom continues on about how late we're going to be.

"But the church is only fifteen minutes away," I argue, strapping on my creased white leather watch. "My watch says we have lots of time."

"Well your watch is wrong," Mom declares stoically.

"But my watch is set to the school's time," I reason.

"Don't argue with me," Mom says.

See, about three years ago, Mom decided to set our living room clock forty minutes fast, I guess to guarantee we'd always be early wherever we went. The problem is, it's the kind of trick that only fools you once. Then you just get into the habit of subtracting forty minutes every time you look at that clock.

Except Mom never developed this habit. She says our living room clock is the exact right time, which drives me and Toni crazy enough to argue with her about it whenever we have to be somewhere on time. And then we turn out being late after all.

Christ United is tucked away in a part of our old neighborhood that you'd never notice if you didn't go there for a specific reason. It rests on a big empty asphalt parking lot hidden inside a circle of houses and trees.

I'm nervous walking inside the church for the first time. Feeling slightly tense and defensive already, I'm bothered by something that doesn't feel right about this church–something that I sense has little to do with praising God.

The first person I see inside the church doors is the last person I'd expect to see; Diane, my goofy best friend from Knightford elementary. I smile with thrilled surprise and run over to tap her "hello" on the shoulder. The next thing you know I'm being introduced to her parents, Mr. and Mrs. Yoakam.

All it takes is for them to invite my family to sit with theirs, and my anxiousness is gone. My mood's turned light. I look over to my Mom to see if we can sit with the Yoakams. Giving a tight-lipped head shake no, she points her finger down at the floor beside her and Toni, signaling me to come stand beside her while the Yoakams go off and take their seats. Being sociable makes Mom uncomfortable.

From out here in the church lobby I can hear the pastor say "everybody shake hands with your neighbor." Mom has us hustle into the sanctuary to find seats now as the service bustles with activity. The standing parish camouflages my sister, me and my Mom as we charge past about ten pews of meeters and greeters. We slide across one of the pews near the front of the church, taking the whole row to ourselves.

I sit down and crack a hymnal, ducking my head to ward off all the open palms coming at me for welcome wishes. With any luck the singing will start up soon. I study the black notes on each score and get ready to sing the dashed words as best I can. The organ hums, offering a sample of the hymn's tune. I follow the lead of some bold voiced old people in the rows behind me.

"Holy, hoooly, hooooleeeeeeeeee…" As I sing, I picture a God that's not so much a person, but more like a presence–a feeling of having company beside you that you just naturally know is wiser and greater and more loving than anything you'll ever be.

The pastor doesn't have the soft face like the one Jesus has hanging on that big cross on the sanctuary wall. He preaches with a chiseled glower, hinting that we all should be prepared for more of a stiff speech than a warm welcome. It gives me a horrible hunch, a thick shiver under my skin telling me his good intentions are as good as gone.

This minister doesn't have the brightness in his eyes that you'd expect a man of God to have. So I watch the man like a hawk; how he stands, when he blinks, if he sings. This pastor is old, but the story he's telling is older– so full of strange names that I have no choice but to lose interest and start scribbling notes to my sister in the margins of my church bulletin.

I can't seem to wholly distract myself from the gist of the minister's message though. It's bothering me, this lecture about good versus evil, saints versus sinners. I almost wonder if this pastor is missing God's point altogether.

I'm not sure what God's point is exactly, but I'm pretty sure it has nothing to do with calling people evil or sinners. I don't have to be religious to know that everyone is good in the eyes of God.

Like my old babysitter Shamarra said, we're all just here to live our lives the best we can, trying to keep a hold on what's good while the bad tries to wash it away in floods. Maybe she should be the one up here ministering to the people.

As the pastor continues his sermon, I feel threatened, uncomfortable, judged. Pounding his fist on the podium, the man makes me involuntarily blink thrice, almost like a stutter of the eyelids. I squirm, fidget, and fiddle with my hands.

"I have to go to the bathroom," I tell my Mom and slide out of the pew without even waiting for permission. I nervously roll up my scribbled program and humbly amble down the side aisle, avoiding all eye contact. I pass ten rows full of people who I know are trying to pin me with the label of sinner just for exiting early.

Just as I reach the usher doors to exit, I take one last look back at the worshipers to see if anyone's turned around to try to figure out why I'm leaving. But everybody's looking straight at the preacher in action. He's slapping a flat hand on his podium and waving the other above his head with determined words about eternal damnation.

In the back of the sanctuary near the church exit my shoe catches on an electrical cord. I thrust forward to keep from falling, pulling the plug out of the wall entirely.

When the pastor's sound system goes mute I realize I'm the cause. Everybody looks around up front, which makes it easier to slip out the rear door.

"Thank you, God!" I say to myself, actually feeling good about leaving that plug sitting on the floor. It's saving all those people from the shame of hearing a lecture.

Walking out of the sanctuary feels like being lifted up onto a cloud of calm. There's a great glass wall at the lobby entrance where a mass of flies dive toward the light outside. About forty flies have already dropped to the floor in a heap of black where I stand.

Shaking off my disgust, I fling myself down the steps toward the basement hoping there's a bathroom down there that locks so I can regroup.

I walk right past a Sunday school class in progress, stopping to peek in out of sheer curiosity. From this distance it looks like Frank is in there. I tune into his voice to see if it's him.

"...The Lord only really has one true rule if ya keepin' track, and that is ta love the world, including everyone in it, at all costs..."

He winks when his eyes tag mine in recognition. I know this is my chance to talk to him, to ask him for direction, or instruction on how to put all the pieces of my life together so I can see a whole picture. But I chicken out, bolting back upstairs, past the flies and the pews full of people. I scoot back beside my Mom and Toni just in time for the organ blasting benediction.

"We were thinking Jenna might like to go with Diane to church camp," Mrs. Yoakam says, greeting us after the service.

"I think Jenna would love that," Mom says, looking at me with a smile. "And that would let me spend some good quality time with Toni."

I eye Mom suspiciously. She's never used the words quality and time together since I've been living.

"Let's go get a donut," I say with impatience, having stirred up some courage to talk to Frank in the basement. Waving Diane and her parents goodbye-for-now, I drag Mom and Toni down the carpeted steps, searching out Frank. Along the way I lose my sister and Mom.

A steady flock of churchgoers sidles around a table of pre-poured cups of coffee and treats. While I wait for Toni and Mom to find me, I try my luck at grabbing a donut. Three adults step in front of me before I get the chance. One of them is a super thin redhead in a jade green dress. She looks shaken and strong, worried but alert. She's holding her coffee cup too tight. By chance I catch a piece of the conversation she's having with a larger woman.

"You gotta understand, Jackie, a broken family leaves cracks for generations..." The lady's speaking to her like there's no one else in the room. "Oh but a healed family—it does the whole world a world of good."

I instantly lighten up at the sound of that. While the conversation continues on, I wonder about the woman, where she calls home, what her life is like. One of them notices me, the heavy-set one. She turns around with a smile.

"A donut please?" I say meekly.

"Oh sorry, we didn't see you there honey. Um, 'looks like they're all gone from the table baby, but I hear there's more in the kitchen. Go on in and ask for one there."

She points to a white door at the far side of the room. I follow the trail her finger drew in the air until the door is before me. I push it open to find Frank standing in the center of the silver kitchen. He pauses from restocking donuts to make a deliberate move to greet me.

"Well look at that, it's Jenna!" he says, casting his powdery hands in the air, making me smile wider than ever.

My skin tingles with heady confidence. He acts proud to know me. If only my family could see it.

"They sent me to get a donut Mr. Frank," I say.

"Is that so? Well, lessee what we can do for ya."

He hands me a chocolate covered éclair stuffed with a yellowy crème, then brushes his hands together.

"Lissen Jenna, I've got work to do now," he says, "But I want cha to promise to come find me when you git back from church camp."

As I nod to him wholeheartedly, I can't help but wonder how he knew I was going.

14

Keep-Away
July Age 11, 1982

It's lightning bug season, the time of year when hundreds of fireflies light up the night, when crickets chirp by the thousands, and when skunks fill the air with the smell of burning rubber.

All the kids on Woodwind Street are going into fifth, sixth, or seventh grade, still young enough to play Keep-Away, Roundup, Kickball, or Flashlight Tag, but also old enough for Bullcrap and Truth or Dare.

The preteen turnout for this Truth or Dare game is by far the largest, nearly filling the ditch that's hidden within a stretch of woods between Woodwind Street and the railroad tracks—a whole territory that kids like us know inside and out, but that adults have never heard of.

"Truth or Dare?" Ricky's a Truth or Dare regular, a kid who'll be going into the fifth grade with me this year. He's always in a hurry to get the game going.

"Truth," I say. I'm a regular, too. Not that I need a game to do dares with boys. I can do that anytime. I play because I want people to know all there is to know about me.

"You always pick truth." Ricky's the opposite of me. He always picks dare—because he wants everybody dry humping. He says it himself.

Ricky's definitely cute, he has a good haircut and a boyish grin; two things that might make me want to hump him someday if his hot temper didn't make him suddenly ugly again.

See, Ricky has these intense moods. He's only ever feverishly happy or fiercely mad, but nothing in between. When he doesn't get his way, you can see the anger begin in his eyebrows, arching high, making blue veins lift off his forehead in the shape of lightning bolts. His flecked nose wrinkles up with flaming contempt. That's when he starts to act wild, snatching our house keys, or anything else we might have with us so he can hold us hostage until he says we can go.

For the last few Truth or Dare tantrums he's had, we girls just scuttled out of the dugout and waited up above in a disinterested way until he felt stupid sitting down there in this giant dirt trench all by himself, like some kind of ogre. But this week, he changed his strategy. He came up out of the ditch and started shoving us back down into it until we finally fought back with kicks and scratches, our best attempt at clobbering him.

And somehow in the middle of it all he did something really weird. He pulled down his pants and dangled his you know what in our faces without even being dared to. That was the day we all told Ricky he could forget about playing Truth or Dare with us from then on and his face got even more nasty looking, like a sun-spoiled rotten tomato.

If there was one good thing about Ricky, it would be that he's the reason I hit it off with the Catholic girl who lives one house down from me. Jennie has joined us a few times for Truth or Dare but I never really talked to her before last night's neighborhood game of Roundup.

I was crouched in the grass hiding behind two closely growing fir trees when she flew around to tag me "it." But instead of tagging me, she tripped right past me, skidding on her palms for at least a foot. I didn't laugh at her, which was hard because she looked so funny falling. Instead, I helped her up and said, "Are you alright?"

"Yeah, thanks. You're Jenna, right?" When Jennie dusted off her fair skin, I realized she could easily pass for my sister. She looked slight like me with a thin frame—basically all legs and lips.

"Yeah, and you're Jennie?" I said making a start beside her to round up the rest of the camouflaged kids. We talked nonstop as we searched for everyone, tittering at the topic of how Ricky's thingy looked like a pig's nose that day he wiggled it in our faces during Truth or Dare.

"You should come up to my house tomorrow," Jennie said, wiping away amused tears.

"Ok." I agreed because I was feeling carefree, relaxed and dangerously impulsive. But I immediately regretted it.

• • •

"Toni, Jenna, you've got to get lost for awhile..." Mom makes her announcement not so much to us, but to the general vicinity of the air inside the house. Her voice trails off as she heads past me, through the living room and towards Toni's room to be sure she heard, too.

"What do I have to do to train you kids to stay quiet at all times?" Mom's wearing a long bathrobe, the one with the singe marks on the sleeve from where she caught it on fire cooking bacon.

"I don't want to hear another word out of either of you starting immediately if not sooner!"

Mom has only been out of bed for fifteen minutes, but she doesn't look the least bit tired. She looks like she's fully charged to go full steam ahead through her day, no matter what obstacle might be in the way.

I've just poured my breakfast cereal onto a dinner plate. I've been doing things like this lately, brainless things. This week alone I put our deli sliced cheese in the silverware drawer, stuck a bag of garbage in the clothes hamper, and somehow managed to shelve my own toothbrush in the hall closet beside the replacement light bulbs.

When your mind starts to flake out on you, you have to wonder if it's checked out on purpose because of the way your life has landed. You find that you're so involved in protecting yourself from circumstances that sometimes you can't see past your own personal desperation, losing your focus completely.

I scurry down to Toni's room so we can figure out a plan for getting out of Mom's hair. My Dad used to call me and Toni army buddies because of the way we clung together like this. He says allies link up their minds and when they do, they become a unified team that's hard to defeat.

"Where are you gonna go?" I ask my sister as soon as Mom retreats toward the living room.

"I guess up to Lynne's," Toni shrugs thumbing the air in the direction of her best friend's house. "What about you?" She knows I get agitated at other people's houses. It seems that being around other people keeps me from making things go exactly the way I need them to go.

"Didn't Jennie invite you over?" Toni prods encouragingly.

She seems intent on making sure I have a plan. That's one good thing about my sister. She makes parts of my life so much easier when she directs me through whatever practical challenge I'm headed towards. When I was first learning how to ride my bike for example, she pedaled ahead of me, calling out instructions. I rode right up behind her, probably too close to her back rim, staying balanced by keeping my focus on her rear wheel. When she pointed out dangers like bumps in the road and sprinkles of splintered glass I knew she was guiding me in the right direction. It gave me a surge of energy, spurring me to ride twice as fast.

Then during those really hard months after my parents divorced, Toni would come home from school every single day telling me "I bet you didn't know blah, blah, blah" teaching me what she learned both in and outside of her classroom so then I would know, too. I gained courage by feeling so much smarter every day, believing that knowing so much information would cast out all the heartbreak.

The thunderous clatter Mom's making in the kitchen is spoiling the very silence she says she needs. I lock eyes with Toni to gauge what to do next. By best estimate, this no talking rule will last until about dinnertime before Mom realizes her mistake and takes it back.

I recall the last time she instructed us not to talk for a whole day. It wasn't until dinnertime that Mom finally called us out of our rooms and over corn and potatoes asked us about our day, as if talking was suddenly the most perfectly normal and welcomed thing to do.

"Ok, I'll go up to Jennie's," I mouth to Toni.

"I'll walk you there on my way up to Lynne's house," Toni whispers, putting up a finger to signal for me to wait for her while she gets dressed.

Toni stretches a band around her hair to make a ponytail as we slip out the front door. I don't know whether or not to tell Mom we're leaving since we're not supposed to talk.

Mom's clamorously stacking pots and pans and scrubbing the kitchen countertops so I decide to just leave quietly. Toni ushers me straight to Jennie's covered concrete porch.

"See you around dinnertime," my sister says, already walking off toward Lynne's, waving at me.

bang, bang, bang

Jennie's aluminum door rattles as I knock. As I wait for an answer, I turn to watch my sister and her own set of problems crest the hill above Jennie's house. I wait five seconds, then ten, pulling my hair back, combing it with my fingers, flicking shed strands of hair to the ground. As the seconds pass, my hesitancy stacks up and up until it tips the scales on the side of doubt.

I exit Jennie's furnished porch in an aimless way, meeting the street, sighing, looking to the sky with relief for not having to stress over a visit. It only takes a few glances left and right, however, to admit to myself that there's no direction to take when you don't know where you're walking. My only option lands me back at Jennie's doorstep. I knock more boldly this time, reminding myself that it can't be as bad as I think it will be. To calm my pounding heart, I call up the picture of me and Jennie running during Roundup, laughing without any effort.

"Come in!"

A smoky adult voice yells from inside. I step onto the first square of carpet tile inside the door and stay there, uncomfortably aware that I'm now standing in a room with Jennie's Mom and nobody else.

Her Mom looks much more relaxed than I could ever imagine myself being. She doesn't seem to care that she's never seen me before. She doesn't even give me a once over. She just keeps stirring what smells like fresh potato salad with her right hand while she holds the phone with her left.

Thank God she's on the phone. I'm sure I wouldn't have known what to say to her if she were free to ask me how I am and how I like living in Knightford Heights. Her Mom is tall, curvy and blond but in an inward, non-flaunting sort of way. She points a mayonnaise-capped finger toward the hallway behind me.

"Jennie's in her room."

Jumping at her apparent command to get lost, I fly around to hurry and go where she tells me to, crashing face first into Jennie who has just walked up behind me.

"Are you alright?" Jennie asks, rubbing her cheekbone. Her round-toothed smile is pearly-white and kind.

"I'm ok," I say through the pulsing pain, concerned that my nose might actually be broken.

"I was just about to get a snack. C'mon."

Jennie leads me in the direction of the refrigerator. Her Mom has since wiped her hands, lit a second cigarette, and stretched the lime green phone cord across the kitchen to take a seat at the table. We duck under the coiled cord.

"Uh huh."

Jennie's Mom holds the phone naturally, like it's an accepted extension of her ear. When she pauses to listen I can hear the *wa wa wa* of the voice on the other end of the receiver.

"That figures, I told you she would," her gossiping Mom says, blowing swirls of smoke out the side of her mouth, idly flipping through the Sears catalog.

Jennie slides open a deep drawer filled with Fig Newtons, Oreos, Fudge Stripes Cookies, Animal Crackers, and Butterscotch Crumpets. And that's only a taste of what's in there. I've never seen such a plethora of choice outside the walls of a grocery store. Jennie produces a pack of Nutter Butters and closes the drawer before I get to see anything more. Handing me a pile of cookies Jennie asks, "What do ya want; soda, juice, iced tea, or lemonade?"

My blood thumps fast in my neck and my eyes dart sideways for fear of such a high stakes question. I hold my breath instead of answering, knowing that Jennie's Mom is about to yell at her for giving out their family's expensive food and drinks to strangers.

"Which one do you want?" Jennie asks me again, patiently holding the refrigerator door wide open, the cool air emptying from the box completely. I take note of any changes on her Mom's face, watching for ticks, squints, winks, or twitches that might warn me that her temper's going to blow. But there's nothing, not even a hint of a sneer. She's so heavily embedded in her phone conversation that she doesn't even seem to notice all the cold air spilling out of her fridge and her grocery bills mounting for all the soda I'm about to hog up.

"Cherry Cola," I say nervously. When Jennie pours our drinks, I watch the liquid level go way down on the soda bottle. My teeth clench down tight as the entire backdrop of the floral pattern on my tall glass turns from clear to cola brown. I gulp the soda down in four swallows and set the empty glass on the counter, knowing it's wrong to be so greedy that I'd actually risk the chance of Jennie getting whipped.

"Mind if I do my chores? I just have to wash these few dishes," Jennie proposes, picking up my empty glass as I nod.

Her family's kitchen sink is yellow and bright. Rich light flows in from the large kitchen windows, giving the whole counter area a nice cheery glow. She stacks up more dishes and silverware from the counter and turns the hot and cold faucets on.

"I'm going to see if there are any more dishes downstairs. Be back in a minute." Jennie says after having dipped her finger in the stream of tap water, I guess to test the temperature. She takes off galloping downstairs.

"Hey, your water's still running." I yell the warning out to no one. Jennie's Mom has since taken to the living room and Jennie's already out of earshot. I stare impatiently at Jennie's running water, thinking about its source. I remember the day we learned in school where our water comes from. I had no idea it was pumped straight out of a lake just outside our city—from something called a reservoir that's home base for plants, animals and fish. I turn the tap off for her, convincing myself I'm doing her a favor. I'm sure she meant to turn it off.

"Hey, did you turn the water off?" Jennie looks confused when she comes back to the sink with the dirty mugs she's collected from the basement.

"I thought you left it on by mistake," I lie.

She turns the tap back on, tests the water temperature, and takes off this time to the bathroom.

"I'll be right back," she says again.

The sapping of the tap drains me somehow. I can almost feel the reservoir's water level plummeting, the fish gasping for water as their habitat gets sucked through Jennie's faucet.

"Look at how much water you're wasting."

I confront Jennie the second she comes back from the bathroom. I feel obligated to speak up for the fish who have to share their water with people who waste it.

"Geez, Jenna. My parents pay the water bill. It's not that expensive."

"You don't even know where our water comes from," I say disapprovingly, crossing my arms.

"Yes I do. The sink," she responds with complete seriousness.

"I forgot. I gotta go." I say with sudden haste. I can feel the heat rising in my face, like I'm being smothered by my intensifying temper. "I'm supposed to be seeing a movie with my friend," I fib, knowing I need instant escape before

I lose my cool completely. I hurry out the door to recover from the desperate need to see Jennie turn off her tap and save the fish.

My blood thrusts from the inside, powering me quickly up the street towards nowhere. I huff and fume at the idea that life can be so free and easy just one house up from mine. I want to be in command of Jennie's waste–to end her carefree enjoyment of the extravagances she lives with. And I want her to help me save the water and the world because I can't save them by myself.

It feels somehow calming and familiar to walk aimlessly up my street. But it's also terrifyingly lonely. A dead end. I take the simplest shortcut to the woods, cutting through a neighbor's empty yard. I dump their water-pooled tire swing as I trudge past, and finally make it back to where their manicured lot turns into forest undergrowth. Creeping carefully past low lying clusters of poison ivy, I find a dense pocket of trees a very far cry from my street.

It feels like a risk–like I'm about to jump off a ledge into the unknown, but I have nothing to lose. Filling my lungs in a deep, nervous inhale, I close my eyes and hold it until I can't hold it any longer. What comes out is a holler that thunders straight past the tops of the trees. I can see myself standing there with my eyes closed, my head tilted back, finding my voice. It's so powerful that it makes all the birds scatter into the sky like winged confetti.

• • •

I can faintly hear footsteps over the thick pulse that's again kicking through my temples. I grab a low branch of a narrow tree trunk outside Frank's church and climb high, branch to branch, my feet finding stepping places in the upside down armpits the tree makes where its branches split. There are tears at the corners of my eyes. The trees are saying, *yes, that's him, don't be afraid. There's telling to do*, they say, and the leaves shiver with patience and understanding.

I prop my forehead on the bark of the strongest and highest branch. This is harder than I thought, finding your voice. It almost makes me feel even weaker, even more lost. I catch Frank just before he walks into the church.

"Help," I say. "It's Jenna."

"I love nature." Frank draws me into his mind without pause, marveling at the sky, the tree, me.

"God didn't make the world so magnificent to feed his ego, I tell ya that. I think it's so breathtakin'. God's gotta *want* us to look all around. He *wants* us to notice things. The world's got beautiful things ta show us."

"But then why do people spoil it?" I search his eyes for the answer, even though I've already mentally incriminated my Mom for throwing Wonder the bird in the garbage and my neighbor Jennie for disorderly water wasting.

"All of nature fits together like a puzzle, would ya agree?" Frank weaves his fingers together in front of his sturdy body to demonstrate. I don't answer him because I'm wondering if he's heard my question.

"Each piece of nature has a very different but equally essential purpose, just like people do," he continues, looking up to me in the high branches.

"But how could there be a purpose to people spoiling nature?" I ask again, shuffling my feet on the bark to get a better grip.

"It's all in the way you look at it, Jenna. Depends if you see the whole spider web or just a single glistening strand. The strand doesn't stand alone, even though the rest of the web might be invisible."

"I don't see what that has to do with people treating nature like trash," I say.

"I think ya forgettin' one thing." Frank taps his temple with his index finger. "*People* are nature, too. Ya getting my point?"

"I don't think so," I say, dangling from the lowest branch of the tree now, feeling the need to stand on my own two feet again.

"Ask yourself this question: 'what would the world be like if the birds convinced the trees to be birds?'"

"So you're saying I shouldn't try to convince people to be like me, even if they're doing something wrong?" I break a small twig from the tree and use it to make the ants hurry along in the opposite direction from me.

"No, I'm sayin' that nobody is right or wrong. Nobody is above anybody else, no one is better and no one is worse because nothing can be without the other. We're all good in God's eyes."

"But what if they hurt you?" I dig in my heels, wanting to be right about this. I thought Frank was going to take my side and help me fix my life.

"Is somebody hurtin' you? Because if they are, it's your job to tell someone ya trust. You can trust me."

"I don't know," I say. "It's more like nobody is *helping* me."

Hanging onto a low leafy limb, I kick my feet out from the trunk and land like a gymnast dismounting on a mat. I squat down on the patchwork lawn and fiddle with a tight clutch of flowers growing from the hard ground.

"Did you know that some flowers hate to be flowers?" Frank says, pointing to my small bouquet of wild violets, kneeling on one knee to get closer to my level.

"Can ya believe that?" He looks at me with wide eyed disbelief. It makes me laugh. "Yes! They *hate* it!" He exclaims with gusto. "They get impatient. They wanna bloom and they wanna bloom *now*."

"Their mistake is," he says, tapping the flower head, "that they think they can only bloom when the conditions are just right. So they wait until the sun is high and long in the day. And then they get ta despise the weeds, tryin' ta claim the sun as their own.

"These flowers never bloom because they're wasting their energy waiting for sustenance, competing, hoping, wishing and praying for fertile loam, ya know, moist ground where there ain't none.

"But lemme tell you a secret. *Some* flowers can bloom without good soil or water or even much sun. They can be all up in a mass of weeds, looking strangled, and they can still bloom big and full and fragrant. Ya know why?"

"Why?"

There's nothing in the universe I want to know more.

"Because they *believe* they can."

My best friend Diane, 1982.

15

In the In-Between
Age 11, August 1982

Diane's Dad stops the family Honda right in the middle of an old wooden bridge that extends over a wide, shallow body of water.

"No one's around for miles," he says. "Let's all get out of the car for a second to look over the railing."

I stretch my stiff eleven year old body out from the cramped back seat and limp on my tingly legs over to the side of the bridge. If I pretend the water isn't moving, it creates an illusion that I'm flying over the water, making me a good kind of dizzy.

I like being here in the in-between, bridged between two divisions of land, between the river's upstream and its downstream, and between yesterday and tomorrow. I imagine that the water coming toward me is the future and the water flowing away from me is the past, washing the years away, far away, and I'm glad to see them go.

This stretch of summer is nonstop hot and heavy. Its steamy temperatures would make a tangle out of most anybody's thoughts, but to Diane's parents the roasting weather inspires a cool stroke of genius. They planned ahead of time to pick me up extra early so we'd have a few hours to spend swimming at the public lake on the way to church camp.

And so with floats in tow, we motor into the lake parking lot, kicking up a row of dust that clusters into one long brown puff. The dust just hangs there above the parked cars, threatening to sprinkle miniscule specs of sand all over the lake visitors' heads. But the lake vacationers don't seem to mind what's looming above them in the least.

Peeling my legs off the sticky car seat is guaranteed to leave a big red oval welt on the back of each of my thighs, but that doesn't bother me as much as the hair at the nape of my neck being stringy and wet.

If a small wish was granted to me right now, I'd be one of those kids who have fancy hair accessories that clip, band or otherwise cinch long hair up and back to sufficiently cool off your collar.

Of course if a bigger wish was permitted, I wouldn't waste it on hair implements. I'd use it to do something really good for all the people of the world and of course for the animals, too.

The dusty breeze kicks up, lifting my hair and rolling through my clothes, puffing my sleeves and shorts cuffs away from my body like I'm inside a temporary hot air balloon. My clothes soften and land back in place when the breeze passes, leaving me with a cooler, yet uncomfortable damp feeling.

With a click, the jaws of the Honda's hatchback yawn open, revealing a pile of sun warmed beach chairs, blankets and swimming gear. Determined to be the one to carry the picnic basket, I skirt around to the back seat to fetch it out first.

The basket, still cool from sitting in the shady spot under the inner tube, is heavy with fruit, sandwiches, carrot sticks, cookies and juice. The forty pounds of food make me lean too far sideways, so I carry the basket against my right leg to usher the weight forward with all the grace of a boar.

"Ya got that?"

Mr. Yoakam asks it in a nice way, but I still feel defensive. I feel the need to prove that I'm stronger than I look.

"Sure, and I can take more, too," I say. And I mean it. I can.

"Looks like we've got it all now. You've got the heaviest thing we have," he says.

Satisfied that my point was made, I stride ahead of the Yoakams with pride, just like the stars in the movies do, carrying a giant picnic basket full of food—only lacking the glittery sunglasses and the chic beach towel that celebrities wear around their necks.

Thank goodness there's actual sand on this beach. What else would keep the Doritos bags, cigarette butts and plastic straws from blowing into the water? The beach blanket Diane's parents brought for us to sit on is enormous. It's a soft purple spread that when laid out intensifies the tan color of the shore. I run my bare feet back and forth over my end of the velvety blanket, delighting in the rare sensory pleasure. Sheer barefoot bliss.

I bet the people around me think I'm a real part of this family, an actual family, with a Mom and a Dad and a sister who go together on trips to have picnics in our bathing suits.

Tons of kids are playing shoulder deep, just short of the bobbing fluorescent orange buoys that block off access to the deepest parts of the lake. The kids can't see it but from this angle on the sand it's apparent there's a fine layer of crust floating on the water's surface. It's just a thin film but crust is crust, so I decide right away that I won't be swimming today. I'll just stay on my towel, no matter how hot it gets.

Mr. and Mrs. Yoakam are a very relaxed couple, but at the same time, they don't waste time dillydallying when it's time to eat a meal. We're only on the beach for two minutes when Diane's Mom starts unpacking our picnic.

I wonder if this is how they describe heaven in the Bible, people parked on beach towels, eating delicious food, looking out towards the line in the distance where blue sky and blue water touch together.

Mrs. Yoakam, looking neither tired nor annoyed with me, gently places a strange looking sandwich in my hands with serious intention.

"I hope you like egg salad sandwiches, Jenna," she pipes, "there's plenty of other food to go around so eat up."

I have no idea what egg salad is but when I taste it, I call it my new favorite food.

Diane makes me laugh all the way through lunch by commenting on everybody who walks by.

"Look at that girl, she's a stick bug in a bikini!" she says about the dark, lanky girl on the towel down by the water. That strikes me as so funny, I clench my lips together and try not to spit out my food. I forgot what it was like to laugh so hard since summer started and I stopped seeing Diane in school every day.

My smile is caked with egg salad, grape skins, carrot chunks and potato chip starch, but who worries about how their teeth look when they're doubled over in fits of giggles? I could never get embarrassed around Diane, anyway, because she would never look down on me.

"Oh my gosh that was so funny," I say, but the words sound more like "Uhmmmmosh rotwmmfmmy" for tumbling over the food in my cheeks. The rest of my chewed food goes down the hatch with a gasp. I gather some air to take my comedic turn next, knowing full well what gets Diane going hysterical.

"Look," I say when a large round woman in a white bathing suit walks by our towel, "there's the biggest whitest pearl I've ever seen outside an oyster."

Buckling and falling on her side with the silent air laughs, Diane is down for the count. With Diane, it's easy to be funny. She laughs at everything. And of course the best thing about being with someone who laughs is that when you're always joking, you temporarily forget that there's any reason in the universe why you'd ever want to cry.

The road to church camp is lined with dark green trees and a thick mulch of ground cover. The place gently leans on my senses and washes away any leftover clogs that might still be blocking the road to my heart. This is the escape from my life that I needed.

There's a row of light yellow shirted male and female camp counselors waiting outside the main cabin to greet us. They look so friendly. I make myself noticed by smiling at them from inside my back seat window, hoping there isn't any egg salad in my teeth.

The camp counselors don't greet us with "Praise Jesus!" like my Grandma says. They just say "hello" and "welcome." One of the female staffers introduces herself as Cinda Sue, a name that matches her southern accent. I like hearing her talk. What's most refreshing is her thought to grab our bags, leaving us freehanded as we follow her up the pinestraw pathway toward the girls' bunkhouse.

The bunkhouse's natural wood floors span its narrow length. The timber walls are lined with rows of neatly made single beds that appear more scattered and haphazard as an assortment of young ladies unpack. Diane and I choose our beds and start unloading our bags, chatting to the girls around us, all of us swatting invisible mosquitoes two seconds too late, trying to scratch away the tingly burning sensation to no avail. Half the legs in this cabin are already covered with the most colossal red bumps I've ever seen.

Mr. and Mrs. Yoakam decide it's time to leave us to our own devices. Walking amid the drone of flies and the nip of the mosquitoes, Diane and I get a good look at the lay of the land, seizing the invigorating punch of the fresh country air, anticipating the companionship of the seventeen Christian counselors.

One hundred campers are now walking in informal lines, arriving at the fire pit from all directions to attend the first scheduled event–the "Icebreaker Bonfire." The fire pit is set up like an ancient amphitheater, rows of lengthy log benches forming a perfect circle around one great blaze.

There's something about a raging fire that can transport you into a mystical mindset. You can find yourself delivered somewhere deep in the tropics, gathering with sages in a primitive time.

Our mysterious looking faces grow warm waiting for the proceedings to begin. We're soon asked to form two large circles so that we can rotate in opposite directions until we have shaken hands and said "peace be with you" to every camper and counselor. Such forced contact with so many strangers gets me feeling antsy in no time. That is until Cinda Sue comes to my rescue.

"Honey, why are you holdin' your breath?"

The counselor from the country extracts me halfway through the greeting round, leading me to a log far from the fire that's ensconced in darkness.

"Is it okay if we talk a minute?" she says. "It's just you and me here. You don't have to say a word unless you want to and nothing you say will be repeated, ever, unless you say it's ok."

She clamps her right hand onto my right shoulder, pulling me in tight to her. "I'm here for you," she says, squeezing my left hand as tight as she can without it hurting.

She's here for me. It's that tiny indisputable piece of encouragement I'd been hoping to hear from an adult more than a few times in my life. Visions of happiness and possibilities run at a steady clip through my mind, one after another, a kaleidoscope of impassioned images.

I gulp and cough in the rhythm of a chugging railroad engine trying to hold my emotions in so I can let some words make their way out. But there are only gasps, breaths, and hiccups of unbelievable relief for being seen. Did the church camp have this plan for their icebreaker, to break the ice on something bigger?

As good as it feels to be seen, my emotional transparency scares me. There's an escalating amount of panic trembling inside, fear of feelings exploding into an embarrassing bawl, a wail, a sob, a shudder.

"I want to tell you a story," Cinda Sue says, assuring me that I need only listen.

"One day when I was about your age the neighbor kids came hustling to my porch, banging on our aluminum screen door, sending my mother in a tizzy and my own cat bolting to the far side of the house. They were yellin' 'Cinda Sue, come quick! There's a cat caught in a trap!'

"You see, I had an easy way with animals in the outdoors. It wasn't something I ever told anyone else. I thought nobody ever saw that part of me. But here I was being asked to rescue an animal whose life was on the line. I was so flattered that these kids read me right that I followed after them, forgetting to put on my shoes.

"I was worried about that cat enough to tramp hard over the brambles that jabbed into my heels along the way.

"When we got to him, I just about cried. He had this long face and tiger striped tail puffed out and smacking the ground. His body was hunkered down on his haunches, as far away from the trap as he could get.

"And then I saw his poor darlin' arm, reaching way out from that big ol' mass of fur that could hardly be mistaken for a cat if it weren't for his growlin' and hissin.' And no wonder he was so mad, his front left paw was nearly split in half by that steel trap.

"So this cat's howling with his eyes stretched wide open. His pupils were just giant, dilated, as they say. There was part of a leaf stuck fast to his eyeball like a contact lens. It was just the most pitiful sight."

"The poor thing! He must've been so scared," I said, already forgetting that she'd pulled me aside to talk about me.

"I know," said Cinda Sue. "And it gets worse. All the kids were standing way too close to the cat, watching him jerk around, suggesting ideas, just talking way too loud. I cut through the bunch of them in my bare feet and told them to step back and be quiet. I inched in there as close as I could get to that moaning mound of a cat. And let me tell you, I was scared as a falling pine cone.

"He clawed me right on the toes, but not before I got a good look at how the trap's metal teeth had snapped tight into his paw, making his claws stick out. It was the most awful mess of bloody fur and broken bones I ever saw.

"Jenna, these kids came to me because they believed I could help. But I had no idea how to save this cat. I couldn't open the trap. And he was howlin' and jumpin', kicking up leaves and dirt, digging into the ground deeper. He kept yanking his trapped paw hard, drawing the chain tighter and tighter."

"So what did you do?" I asked Cinda Sue, hopefully.

"The only thing I could think of. He'd pulled the chain so tight, I had to give him some leverage. I unhooked the chain from the tree but I didn't hold it tight enough. The cat gave a tug in this knee jerk spurt that made me lose my grip. He took off through the woods—faster than I'd ever seen an animal run. He ran and ran through the woods with that steel trap on his paw and a long chain trailing behind him. I felt awful. There were so many things I wished I had done differently. And I'd like to hope that the cat was found by somebody who could help him, but I'll never know."

"You didn't find him?" I asked, deflated.

"No, I tried to run after him, we all did, but he was gone like a flash of lighting. None of us ever saw him again. If I had the chance to do it over, I would have called someone who was experienced to help, I would've made all the other kids go away, and I would've taken the time to put my shoes on.

"I'm not telling you all this to upset you, Jenna. It's just to show you that sometimes things happen in life, horrible things that we're not prepared for. And because those things hurt our hearts, we want so badly to fix them. But we can't always make everything better."

"But you can't just *leave* things," I say, drawing out the word leave to point out that it's the worst thing in the world to do.

"That explains why you were holding your breath," she says, slapping her knees, thinking she's gotten a grasp on what makes me tick. And she's right. She has.

"Jenna, what do you do when you've tried to make everything better and it's not working?"

"I keep trying," I say, proudly.

"But what do you do when you get tired of trying?" She asks compassionately, deliberately.

"I keep trying anyway," I say, putting my hands over my eyes to hold in the tears. She knows.

There's something about hearing things out loud that make them so much more real.

"That's a whole lot of burden for one little girl to carry," Cinda Sue says clutching my shoulder gently with thoughtful understanding.

I jerk from her touch involuntarily, startled by the compassion, the sympathy, the freedom from guilt for not being able to save the world; my family; my self. A waterfall of emotion spills down onto mushrooms and leaf litter. The familiar smell of my skin and the warmth radiating from my palms help me think through my tears.

"I like that you're crying with me. Nobody should make a practice of feeling their feelings all alone. It can get too scary for one person."

"How did you know?"

"-that you carry the world on your shoulders? You're not the only one who can pick up on people's feelings," she says, stroking the hair out of my eyes with her free hand.

Jenna, keen awareness is a great gift. You can use it for good things. You have an extraordinary ability to calm and comfort people just by being understanding and warm, like a blanket."

"Yeah, but that's where I get stuck. I don't feel very warm."

"Maybe that means *you* need a blanket," she says, a slight bit worried. "Let me be clear about something. I'm going to need you to look me in the eyes when I tell you this because I need you to really hear me when I say it.

"Jenna, people like you and me can get pulled into the world's problems faster than a snake swimming in a river. That's why you and I have to be vigilant. You know what I mean by that? It means it doesn't matter what anybody says or does, wants or needs. Before you can save anyone else, you have to first become a master at taking care of yourself."

"How do I do that?" I say, eager to finally be getting my wish for instructions on life. "I'll do anything. Just tell me what to do."

"First and foremost, you have to do some clean up work."

Cinda Sue picks up a stick and draws a tall line in the dirt. I can barely see it in the muted glow of the fire pit. "You need some solid ground to build on. It's going to sound funny, but this is the very most important step. You can't skip it."

"What is it?" I ask impatiently.

"You're going to have to let your heart break, Jenna. You'll have to let out all the feelings you've ever held inside spill right out in the open. It's called being honest about who you are and what you feel. The only thing wrong with having feelings is trying to pretend you *don't* have them."

"But I…"

"Now make sure you feel your feelings with someone who will keep you safe and comforted. If you don't know anyone who could do that, you might write your feelings down on paper, or let your tears spill in the outdoors. But it's very important that you are not doing this without some kind of support. You absolutely need to tell someone what you're doing. Just make sure it's someone safe–who you know you can trust, like a teacher who's nice or a friend's parent."

"I don't know anyone I would feel like telling. Except one person at my new church. And you." I say, doubtfully.

"See? There's two more people than you knew before, right?" She laughs. She has a pretty laugh. I think I know what she means. She's looking at it like today is a new day and I can make tomorrow into anything I want.

The morning sky spreads a cool layer of dew over the warming camp countryside. Diane and I walk with the other campers along a wide woody forest pathway toward a place called Eagle Outdoor Amphitheater. Hundreds of butterflies color the road before us, their fragile wings flapping like clicks of light in the filtered sunshine.

I feel lighter than the wind today, like there are real wings on my back. The life I deserve is right out in front of me, in plain sight. I'm inclined to believe the river we crossed on the way here really did carry away my past.

Things are turning around.

On the hot drive home, I wonder if I'm more prepared for my life back in Riverston. Could life really become something effortless, something to even look forward to?

A rumble shakes me from my thoughts. My mosquito bites pulse and burn. I scratch them hard for that fantastic moment of itch soothing bliss. We're crossing that bridge again.

This time I only get a quick look out the car window over the expanse of water that's rushing under us. I feel a current of love inside me. Cinda Sue, the other camp counselors and the other campers still stand clearly in my mind, reminding me to keep moving ahead. There are good things to come.

My Dad in his apartment, 1984

16

Slipping
Age 13, 1984

Sometimes when I look at my thirteen year old reflection in the mirror I can see a million kids like me filed away in normal looking homes across the country, maybe the world. We're all searching for something we're missing, so serious, so young.

Something happened to our household over the last two years. It felt like shifting gears in the middle of driving. Frank got forgotten and church wasn't working. Toni and I began dating and babysitting. We were introduced to Mom's boyfriends and Dad's girlfriends. Mom got tough on punishment and switched to working with juvenile delinquents. Dad stayed distant. Toni tried smoking. I exploded with temper tantrums.

I demonstrated my idealistic convictions by recycling, saving energy and becoming vegetarian. Met with retaliation for my ecological rebellion, Mom required me to do my own shopping and cooking. All in all, the truth was glaring. The help I'd wished for still wasn't coming.

This year I can't imagine that anything will be different. If I'm confident about anything it's that my lifeboat is sinking.

"Where are the scissors and why is your door closed?"

Mom's commotion tends to begin first thing every morning.

"Don't be snappy with me."

Mom lords over my bed, arguing with the fearful glare I'm giving her for the way I've been awakened.

"What? I didn't even do anything," I say, rubbing my eyes.

And I realize she's done it again. She's sucked me in.

"Then why didn't you answer me?" she reasons. "What did you do with the scissors? They aren't in the drawer."

"They should be. I just saw them there last night."

I know it's best to reassure her. I'm determined to be good, to not get punished.

When Toni and I get punished, we have to watch out for each other, to defend against Mom's unpredictable emotional rises and falls. We help one another feel safe, trying together to make our home life run as normally as possible.

Not long ago, Toni had the idea that we could decorate our rooms to make them feel more like private territories of escape and promise. She said we should fill our walls with clippings and creations of our dreams and desires—things that represent what we love. It was a great idea, and even though we found out that it takes a long time to think about what you love when you're not even sure who you are, we managed. We got our rooms done the way we wanted them to be. And they looked like somebody lived in them, unique kids who had creativity and dreams for a good life.

I plunge back onto my pile of pillows while Mom darts dynamically down the hall, rolling open the bathroom drawer to look for the scissors, shuffling through it in an almost unrestrained manner. Her agitation scares me, my anxiety climbs.

I think of Frank, trying to call on some advice he would have for me at this very moment.

"Think of your troubles as a sharpening stone," I remember him saying before I last left him "grinding against your rough edges, smoothing you out, making you into a jewel."

"But my problems make my edges rougher, not smoother," I told him, feeling truly ground and splintered, like more of a pencil than a diamond.

"I 'spose you need some more exposure to the elements first," he said.

Not knowing what he meant, I pictured myself sitting between massive rounded stones deep in a shallow stream like the ones my Dad used to take us to, letting the icy water wash over me for years on end, preparing to emerge someday beautifully, as finished as a fine diamond.

I must've drifted to sleep for a second, maybe halfway started dreaming, until the sound of shouting mixed with the clean tearing of paper sounds from my sister's room across the hall. *Rrrrrrrrrip.* Shrill. Jolting me awake again.

"What're you doing?" Toni's voice is closer to pleading than asking.

"There shall be no expression of compromised ideals in this house," Mom shouts at my sister. As smart as I am, I don't think I exactly know what Mom's trying to get at. But there is one thing I do know. When she uses big words in a robotic way, her temper has boiled over. I clutch my warm covers, stuffing them around my ears.

"You're grounded until I say otherwise." I can hear Toni's punishment being announced from the other room. I imagine that Toni's brow is wrinkled and her lips are pursed; her tongue is probably poised to argue the nonsense of it all.

"In fact, you're both grounded." Mom expands the punishment to include me, though I haven't even been out of bed yet today.

I know by now that there's no use in arguing with my Mom. There's no reasoning and no calming. I just have to stay quiet and wait for her fury to burn out. Listening for a clue of what to do next, I stay frozen in my bed looking stone-faced, feeling as shredded as Toni's posters that are surely now scattered in pieces all over her bedroom floor.

Mom retreats to the kitchen, cooling off her temper by dialing my Dad to vent. We don't see Dad so much anymore, and I hate to wonder what he might be thinking when Mom calls him up to tell him her distorted version of what just happened.

"The girls are causing big trouble here," she says into the mouthpiece. "They're having temper tantrums. They're destroying their own rooms."

Time stops like a punctuation mark at periods like this. The punctuation is a momentary exclamation, a red underscore, telling you, "Look here. Stop and really look at this scene." The pause in time lets you recover a little, and learn something by studying all the characters in the production—what their faces are showing, how they're framed, where they're headed.

You can see Mom lying, Dad shrugging, sister stewing and me hiding and that shows you how ridiculously dramatic it all seems. At least for that tiny blip in time, you might understand that the chaos is just there to conceal the truer picture—a picture of humanness and vulnerability—a portrait of a family that's fighting a villainous yet heroic battle for some indefinable sense of serenity, drifting aimlessly but rowing, rowing, rowing hard, separate but together in the same sinking boat.

Age 14

17

Life as a Canary
Age 14, 1985

Our new family counselor is a sandy haired middle aged man wearing a casual suit. He stands amidst a living room scene of sofas and chairs, lamps and tables. Mom's brought us here because she says we're out of control. Says we're making a mess of the family.

I trace my first initial in a layer of dust on the reception counter, thinking about how everything shifts, cracks, gathers dust, turns or changes at times, and how those shifts can really affect my mood. Maybe I should tell the counselor that I need to keep things in good order all around me or I can't breathe.

Back at home, there's a jumble of knickknacks cluttering up our counters, floors, and shelves, crowding me out. I feel the need to rearrange the porcelain figurines, clay pottery, crystal vases, and plastic potted plants so they're balanced, in separate but equal spaces within the house. It isn't easy seeking out abandoned corners, shelves and cubbyholes where so many objects can sit with a little breathing room so they can be better viewed and more properly valued. I can't rest until deep pools of water are dumped from the bathroom soap dish, scrunched rugs by the doorways are fixed, wax is melted to fix leaky candles, and stacks of magazines are staggered so they won't slide to one side.

When I was younger, my Mom said I was like the girl in *The Princess and the Pea* where the princess feels a tiny pea through twenty mattresses and can't sleep. And when she told me the story, the pain of the pea pressed into my own back.

"That poor princess!" I said.

"I swear, Jenna. You're so sensitive they could put you down in a mine instead of a canary," Mom remarked.

I took it as a compliment, thinking she was saying since I was as cheerful and bright as a canary, I could take the bird's place anywhere. But since then I found out that when you put a canary down in a poisoned mine, it's so sensitive that it'll drop dead, telling miners of a fatal gas that they couldn't otherwise see. I hope that doesn't mean I'll drop dead before I can save my family and the fellow beings of the world from the deadly dangers lurking around in our midst.

This counselor man invites the three of us to take a seat anywhere in the office, trying to make us feel at home. I honestly don't know if I would recognize that feeling if I felt it. I balance on the edge of the counselor's sofa feeling strange to be off the floor and at level with everyone else. My form is rigid, knees clamped tightly together. My hands are folded on my lap.

"Go ahead. Sit back and relax, Jenna," the man says. "We'll be here for a while."

Sitting back with ease feels risky, but I take the chance.

"I have a master's degree in social work and fifteen years experience with a practice in Tampa…"

When the counselor talks way too long about himself and his qualifications, I pretend I'm heavily weighing his words by wrinkling my forehead and nodding with mock interest. But all I'm thinking about is Mom's empty pocketbook. *Twenty minutes have passed. How many dollars is that?* I make a list in my mind of things Mom could buy me with the money we're spending on this guy who's not helping. School clothes. A set of pens. A fresh stick of deodorant...

"Ok, before we get started, I'll need you to fill out some forms," he says, clicking his ballpoint pen.

My pen doesn't write, so I just look at the blanks and checkboxes that ask you for your name, age and what you know about your family history. I don't know anything about my family's health, anyway. I look down, swirling the dead pen on the paper, pretending to be writing.

The counselor collects our papers, folds his hands and with all neutrality, asks who wants to talk first. My Mom volunteers, pulling out from her overstuffed purse a long list of complaints about how out of control Toni and me are.

"I want them to shape up," Mom says, folding up the paper and sliding it under her leg when she's done reading it, as if someone's going to snatch it and prove she's guilty of deceit.

The therapist then gives my sister and me a glance and says he's going to give us a turn to say what we're feeling.

"This is an opportunity to air your feelings about what life is like for you in general," he says. "You can say anything that comes to mind. Try to focus on how you feel," the counselor coaches.

This is the moment I realize that you have to always be ready for what you wish for. Now that the opportunity has finally come, I'm not prepared with an answer. How do I put my inner world into words? I sit completely speechless. And for once, Toni's lips are sealed, too.

Maybe we've said all we needed to say with our silence. Because by the end of the session, the counselor asks Mom if she wouldn't mind scheduling some solo appointments to help her "work through some things."

I know what that means.

Help has finally arrived.

• • •

"George's moving in with us tomorrow," Mom declares, bursting into my room without knocking after returning from her first solo counseling session.

Mom has been steadily seeing this guy George for six months now. I've steadily been seeing right through him, hoping one day Mom would see through him, too. And break up with him. It's not because I still want my Mom and Dad to get back together, either. Believe me I've long since given up on that ever happening.

"Toni, did you hear what I said?"

Mom whisks towards Toni's room, putting her earrings on as she talks. I duck past her through Toni's doorway and tuck my body in tight at the corner of Toni's bed, ready to join forces with her if need be. Toni's evidently too absorbed in her teen magazine to react to my presence.

"Great. My life's already miserable. Why not invite George into the mess." Toni pipes up without looking up, appearing to be making progress on reading her magazine. She hates George too.

"It's best that you learn about how to cope early in life. It can only help you later on," Mom says for the umpteen millionth time. "And give me that magazine."

Toni and I exchange looks of disgust.

I try to remember what Frank said about every person being important in their own way. Maybe George will fit in to our house just fine. I get a light feeling when I think of Frank's kindness and optimism. He taught me to see the best in people–to give them the benefit of the doubt. Who knows, George might even lighten Mom up a little.

"Scram!"

Mom makes a sweeping motion with her hands in the direction of our rooms when George's black convertible mustang glides into our driveway, rumbling loud.

"Let George settle in for a few minutes before you come out for dinner."

Toni, Grandma and me know by now that when Mom issues an order, you dive into action or else. Grandma makes a run for her room first, scuttling away as fast as she can. The three of us ultimately collide shoulder to shoulder, forming a clog in the narrowest artery of the hallway, all vying for escape from Mom, who's now walking up behind us clapping her hands together, prodding us along.

"C'mon, Go, Go, Go!"

Grandma's squared heels drag against the green shag carpet enough to make friction, shocking me every time I come in contact with her electrically charged dress.

I'm fourteen now, still the smallest, so the first to break free from the three person jam and arrive in the safe zone, my bedroom. Toni scrambles into my room behind me, old army buddies. We lie side by side on our stomachs like old times. Except Toni and I can't sit still for long. We're programmed to keep busy after years of hearing about how there's too much to do to always be lounging around. Everybody knows you're wasting your life if you're not making the best of your time, working hard, getting things accomplished.

"Let's rearrange your room," Toni says. "We can hide your trash can here and move the bed this way so you can face the window…"

With a great whomp, George flops his suitcase down on the living room floor. George gives me the creeps. It's not what he wears to work at the County or that he stands with his toes pointing out. I don't mind that he's built pretty similar to my Dad but smells oddly like an auto shop. What bothers me is that his heart is not detectable by even my most discerning radar.

Still, I call out a greeting as loud as I can from my bedroom way down the hall. I think it's important to say "hi" and "how are you" to make a person feel welcomed. After all, it must be hard to be moving into a strange house.

But George doesn't answer me. And I know he heard me because I can hear him say, "How about a nice glass of Coke?" to Mom. And I can also hear Mom jumping to it, clinking ice in a glass and *hsssst*, opening a hissing soda bottle.

"Girls, Mother, can you come out here?" Mom calls the three of us from our rooms sooner than expected. "I want to give you a new tour of the house," she says once we've gathered in our shrinking living room. "There will be a few changes since George is the man of the house now."

Smiling to George, Mom nods in his direction. "See this half of the couch? It's now George's seat. You should never sit in it, even when he's not home." Mom produces the news with a hand on her hip, and a finger in the air.

Then with a strange sounding grunt that seems odd even to Mom, George sits down to demonstrate how he will be occupying his new spot on the couch. He kicks both his shoes off, sending them flying in the direction of our feet.

Even though I've known George for six whole months, I had no idea that all this time he's been hiding a whole garbage dump under each sock. George's stocking feet project a funk so toxic into the air that the furniture around it could very well disintegrate. You'd think a person would be begging for forgiveness for emitting such a smell, especially right before dinner. But George seems almost proud of his rankness, happily heaving his smelly feet up on our side of the couch with no self-consciousness whatsoever.

With no place to sit, Grandma, Toni and I stay standing in limbo, wanting to hold our noses, hoping Mom will quickly tell us what to do next.

"Dinner's ready! C'mon George."

George waddles in his low hung oil-stained jeans, past the three of us, toward Mom's delicate white padded antique chair that's strangely situated at the head of our dinner table. I know the value of that chair better than anyone. Mom shelled out two hundred and fifty dollars for it two years ago when she knew full well I needed new shoes.

"Wait, you can't sit there," I warn, distinctly remembering the lady at the antique store saying it was for looks only.

"That chair," I address George with uncharacteristic frankness "is not made for sitting. Ask Mom." Mom has never even let herself sit in that chair. Ignoring my warning, George thuds down on it, picking his teeth.

"Mom!" I yell, telling on George. I deserve to have that chair more than George does, because I would treat it so delicately it would last forever like antiques should.

"Jenna go sit down."

Mom's tone is agitated. Her patience is getting short. I guess I should be happy for the wobbly chair I have to sit in now. It's at least one step up from where I sat all through elementary school.

"Why are you sitting in a high chair?" I'll never forget how Theresa Boggs silenced everyone at my tenth birthday party with this direct question. Back then I was the new kid in school. And my twelve closest classmates were waiting for my answer. So naturally I did the only thing I could do. I jumped up out of the chair as if I wasn't sitting in it.

"I don't know," I said touching the back of my neck with my right hand, crossing my legs together. Up until that day, I thought every ten year old kid sat in a high chair at home. I thought it was an honor to be so small that you still fit in your original high chair. Mom said so.

Squeezing between Mom's chair and the wall to get seated for supper, I realize for the first time how much extra effort I've spent all these years for the sake of everyone else's convenience. My spot at the table, and in the family, has been at the far corner of anyone's concern.

As the most perceptive one in the family, I've always stayed keenly aware of the needs of others, making sure to take the least amount of space, be the quietest, give up the good seats, eat the leftovers, and make use of the hand-me-downs everybody else is too good for. I must've gotten so used to wanting the best for everyone else that I've picked up the habit of choosing the worst for myself.

Knock, knock, knock. Toni steals away from the table with her pork barbecue sandwich in hand, leaving her homemade French fries and chocolate milkshake to rest while she answers the door.

I sip my chocolate shake, imagining it's someone coming with a message for me, a telegram from God saying sorry we made a mistake and a swift correction is in order. We're taking you to your real planet now. But Toni comes back to the table as quickly as she left, with half of her sandwich gone already, announcing with her mouth still full that it was just the neighbor kid looking for her lost dog.

"I hate kids," George laughs, looking out of the sides of his squinty eyes like we're all in on some joke. "They always come to your door right at suppertime."

Toni and I lock eyes. *Hate kids?* That makes me want to take my plate and my shake and go eat in my room, but that would mean I'd have to suck in my breath and squeeze behind Mom's chair again. I glance at Grandma to see her reaction to what George just said. She's sitting sweetly in her own world, looking mighty thin actually, and pale, eating a few bits of pork with her fork.

Mom laughs along with George who just said he hates kids right out loud.

"Toni and I are kids, too you know," I want to stand up for myself, "kids who are sitting right in front of you if you haven't noticed." But instead, for some terrible reason, I laugh along with him, too. I don't know why I do it except that "I hate kids" is the first thing he's sort of said to me since he moved in a whole half hour ago. And so I should encourage him. After all, it's a start.

Watching TV is next on the agenda, the best way to avoid after-dinner conversation. With a static 'chink,' the TV comes to life, somehow sucking more of mine away. Toni doesn't seem to mind watching television, but I can't help but remember when it used to feel different after dinner.

A long, long time ago my Mom and Dad would take us outside in the grass to digest our meals. Me and Toni would sit on their laps after supper, filled with food and feeling full of life. Sometimes when the light of midsummer blanketed our late evening neighborhood, they'd carry us on their shoulders to the playground and push us on the swings for a spell. I just could feel their hearts wide out in the open in those days. But like I said that was a very long time ago.

George stops clicking the remote control at the worst possible place—a crime scene with dark crimson blood on dirty city streets, death brought to life by spinning blue police lights. I look at Mom with wide eyed anxiety, waiting for her to tell him to change it.

George, change the channel, will ya?

I try to send the message telepathically.

George?

Mom?

George?

I focus my eyes on the bits of fuzz and string that have landed on the carpet since I last vacuumed so I don't have to see the people in terror on the screen. But the TV just seems to boom louder when I look away. The screaming and cursing swallow up any possible feeling of peace that the room had the chance of giving me. And the hum of the dramatic violins and high pitched horns are sure hints that more atrocities are yet to come. My heart pounds hard. I close my eyes, cover my ears.

Mom.

Say.

"Stop."

People aren't built to watch crimes. They're meant to stop them. This TV show feels too real. Because it is real. This stuff really happens in the world. I want to stop the crimes that are spilling into my living room. But I don't know how. So I'm left with a filthy feeling in my veins.

George, Mom, aren't your hearts pounding, too?

Your hearts?

No don't tell me.

I don't want to know.

Because I already know.

Jenna, fight or flight?

Flight.

• • •

When George walks out on Mom a few months later, I dust off my hands and say to myself with relief and gladness, "Well, that's that." But layered on top of my joy is Mom's sadness. I can't feel my good feelings if she's not happy. So there's just one thing to do.

I have to convince George to come back. It will be easy. And who knows, I might even be my Mom's hero. I sit down at my desk, pull out a sharp pencil, a sheet of notebook paper, and write:

Dear George,

My Dad doesn't believe there's a God. He says science doesn't have any real proof. Mom says that's why they call it believing, because you're never going to have any real proof. But I think there is real proof. The proof is in people who have families they can count on. The proof is in people who love each other. And I think there's a million other ways that proof of God might be seen. Like when two people decide to come together to fix what's broken.

I think that God made human hands fit together because we're meant to hold on to each other. If we were to speak with God, that would be just what me and

Toni and Grandma and Mom would ask him for. Please come back.

Sincerely,
Jenna

When George comes back, he never mentions the letter. He just shows up one day after work like he never disappeared. And he and Mom get along okay that way. Except when they don't. And when they don't get along, Mom needs us to fix it. She says we kids have to try harder, do better, be more, so George will want to stay. And just so we don't forget, she's made some reminders, handwritten messages in blue ink on torn squares of paper, scotch taped on select places around the house.

"Do not leave this cupboard door open or George will bump his head."

"This TV remote control is for George only."

"Do not throw away George's car magazines."

"Keep porch light on for George."

"Keep Coke cold in fridge for George."

Day in and day out, the messages badger me, making me wonder how my life would be different if my own name were printed on the papers in place of George's.

As the year rolls on, a growing plethora of messages make their way beyond the painted kitchen cupboards, the felt covered furniture, and the aging electronics toward the bathroom tile, and down the hallway wall.

The peculiar pieces of paper creep closer and closer to me, Toni and Grandma's bedrooms, telling us, hey you have to keep on top of another one of George's needs.

George's needs.

George's needs.

My room is the only place I can escape the messages, so I spend more and more time here under the covers, safely sandwiched in my bed. I want to come out of my room, but first I have to feel good about doing it.

When I'm alone in my room I think about how passing time might make you look older on the outside, but it can't guarantee any change on the inside. Just like crossed bridges don't necessarily get you anywhere if they're leading you around on a circular road. Nothing about life magically gets you anywhere on its own accord. You have to help it along.

So I fill my chest with air and dare to dream of something better for myself. I conjure up a crisp picture, filling it with great details about how I want my life to look and feel way into the future–a time where the taped handwritten messages of my past have long since faded, gotten brittle and crumbled to dust, erasing any evidence of a stranger's needs ever having been put before mine.

18

The Point System
Age 15, 1986

I remember the day we watched the space shuttle Challenger take off, then explode on TV during class. It was the day I needed to meet somebody just like Ashley.

"Don't call me," she said, handing me her phone number after we discovered an instant friendship in the high school cafeteria lunch line, discussing the awfulness of the space shuttle disaster. "I'm not allowed to get phone calls. I have to wait 'till my Dad goes to work to use the phone."

I glanced at the unusable phone number, relieved to find a comrade whose friend to friend communication is just as proscribed as mine. It's a terrible thing to be glad about, I know, but every bit of misery needs some company.

Ashley is a stylish and popular brunette who wears fashionable accessories in a casual, non-pompous way. When you talk to her, she seems surprisingly honest, not at all concerned with what people will think of her. She just does and says whatever she wants, like telling people personal things about her home life.

"My Dad's a policeman," she tells me while steadily removing her left contact lens using the girls' bathroom mirror. "Actually, he's a crazy racist. It's ludicrous the way he acts."

I get a good look at her reflection, getting familiar with her lightly made up hazel eyes. A friend's eyes. Ashley blinks fast in the mirror. It comes to mind how Frank helped me keep going the few times I've needed him over the years. I don't know why I've stayed out of touch with him for so long.

I hope Ashley has someone like Frank.

I pinch my right gold hoop earring and look to the side, deciding to replenish my red lipstick in the mirror next to Ashley's.

"We should get together more," I say, remembering a day when my anxious shyness would have prevented such a suggestion.

"We should," she says, inspecting her braces. "Unfortunately I'm not allowed to go anywhere except for school and work," she says, puckering her lips now to check their gloss level, almost kissing the mirror. "My Mom sneaks me out sometimes but my Dad doesn't want *her* going out anywhere, either."

The notion of her Mom having restrictions gives me a quick shiver and a picture of a world peppered with women living like that, prisoners in their own homes.

"So your Mom's grounded, too?" I smile, trying to make a joke to shake off the troubling thought.

"And get this," Ashley goes on to confide more to me, gracefully ignoring my inappropriate joke. "Me and my brother can't watch any TV shows with black people on them. Yesterday my Dad caught me watching Oprah and said, 'Get that black lady off the TV.'"

Ashley's confession sends me into spontaneous fits of giggles. It could be my nervousness making me laugh when I'm supposed to be serious. Or just relief at finally meeting someone who understands what it's like to live with rules that make no sense.

"I can't imagine having to change Oprah," I say soaping my hands in the sink. "But here's a better one. When I'm grounded, my Mom takes the phone and the TV with her to work when she leaves."

I splash water for effect when I say it, letting her know she's lucky to be getting to watch anyone on TV, even if it is only white people.

"Wow."

"I know. That's what I'm saying."

For the rest of the school year, Ashley and I blend into one person, never finding ourselves apart inside or outside of school. We ride the same bus, work the same job and share the same clothes. I write her notes and wait for her before getting in the lunch line. She lends me money when I leave mine at home. We share secrets, laughs and tampons.

And sometimes we share some humble refuge.

I need it especially today. When my Mom unhinges completely I can't run to Ashley's house fast enough. As I run, I think about the people near the Chernobyl power station in the wake of their nuclear accident. I have never lost the mental image of people getting X-rayed as they ran during a fictional nuclear war in the TV movie The Day After. It spooked me terribly.

Around the same time the movie aired, I was reading a book about a girl named Sadako who got leukemia because of the 1945 Hiroshima, Japan atom bomb. She'd missed her goal of folding 1000 paper cranes for luck. Her friends finished the project for her, and her hope lived on.

I guess I'm luckier than some right now. I'm not dying or escaping a holocaust or a war. I try to keep it all in perspective, but I can't deny that years of accumulated stress does become truly traumatic. It's draining taking stab after stab at exterminating a mushroom cloud of ruin that's swelling, especially when you're not sure if there will ever be an ending.

Pat, pat, pat.

The steep slope transports me quickly, aiding my flight. Ashley's house is in sight within minutes. Going through her front door is asking for trouble. Her Dad's home and he's made it known he'd get his gun if unwelcome company comes. Ashley's bedroom window is my only hope. I toss cracked cement from around the house's perimeter against her window to get her attention.

"Hey Jenna, what happened?" She slides the window open, whispering, concerned, not surprised.

"It got really bad today. I ran away."

"Oh no, Jenna. Ok. Hold on. Let me think...Ok, I can sneak you in the basement when my Dad gets in the shower up here. My Dad's going to be leaving for work in about fifteen minutes so once he leaves we can talk and figure something out. Don't worry. Just go around back. I'll let you in."

I slip nervously into her barren backyard past the weedy air conditioning unit, feeling infected with an incurable case of trepidation, one suspended sinking feeling. Ashley's opened her back door for me, causing her family's brown dog to bark hoarsely, repetitiously, as if hinting that the house I'm about to step into is no less chaotic than one I just escaped.

I shilly-shally back and forth before the open door, leaving Ashley to keep holding it. Stepping back, I look up to the windows on the outside of the house, seeking some kind of declaration from the higher floors that will help me establish whose house is more dangerous, hers or mine.

"Hurry up!" Ashley hisses, holding the barking dog back.

"I'm coming," I declare, stepping inside.

"Who's at the door?" Ashley's father's words shoot out through the air from upstairs like four stray bullets. He has a deep southern accent and a gruff voice.

At that instant the weight of the house's emotional burden casts a cloud of gloom upon me, hanging invisible but substantial like a great weighty hex. This was a mistake.

"My Dad's getting in the shower right now," Ashley says, signaling me through her basement past her lounging brother who's watching white people on TV. He silently mouths hello to me like it's normal to see people sneaking past him. I can hear the shower kick on upstairs. I timidly let Ashley guide me up, treading through tension on tiptoes.

A threadbare kitchen carpet leads us past a large table that's covered with an array of yellowing starches; a tray of lasagna, a platter of ripple cut French fries and a bowl of potato salad. It looks like there's just been a potluck dinner at the house but only Ashley's family showed.

Ashley's Mom, who's cleaning up the kitchen, turns to give us an almost imperceptible signal that the coast is clear. Through the smoky living room we go, past her Dad in the bathroom and at last into Ashley's room. But the pressure I feel still perseveres. It's like the danger of her Dad somehow still seeps out of the bathroom and under Ashley's closed bedroom door to give me the worst case of the creeps.

Ashley presses her ear to her door, listening on full alert for sounds, movement, changes. The shower cuts off.

"Hide in my closet."

Ashley suddenly shoves me onto a pile of boxes and laundry just beneath a row of jangling wire hangers. Her closet is stuffed with a great jumble of sheets, clothes, dog toys and hair curlers. School books, makeup, pens and pencils, pocketbooks and pictures form a mosaic blanket over every surface of the rest of her room. I feel like I belong in this untidy heap because of my inner clutter, a mishmash of conflicting thoughts littering the confines of my mind.

At the same time, the disarray makes me sweat with overwhelm, calling up distressing products of past experiences, severe fears and vexing reservations. I check the crevice in Ashley's closet door which offers a porthole view of her actions. She's cleaning up her room, kicking a few leftover odds and ends under her bed to distract herself.

Feeling claustrophobic, I scratch my neck. It's begun to burn with great big hives, reacting to the matter at hand. Exactly when will Ashley let me out of her higgledy-piggledy wardrobe?

The rash on my neck is what the doctors call psychosomatic, as in imaginary. My body has always reacted to my thoughts and emotions, burning with a feverish fire at my angriest times, turning pale to the point of ghostliness when I feel my deepest disappointment. But the doctors say to just ignore the symptoms because they are just in my head.

Like the day after Mom and Dad's divorce when I sprayed on too much perfume at the mall and blacked out. The doctors told my Mom it was just an anxiety attack, a mere spell of nervous tension. "Nothing to worry about," they said, "Just ignore it." And they sent us home.

When you live like Ashley and I do, you learn fast to be extremely accurate, acting only on facts, striving to get all the details right, not daring to risk messing up.

"My Dad has to be at work in fifteen minutes, so hang tight," Ashley says after listening out her bedroom door once again. And so, precisely as predicted, Ashley's Dad's police car does indeed scream down the street minutes later, sounding like an emergency in the making. The itchiness on my neck ebbs that very instant.

"Ok, come out, Jenna."

Ashley snatches a travel pack of Kleenex from a stray pocketbook lying under her bed and hands it to me as I emerge.

"I can't take it anymore," I say, crackling the plastic package of tissues in my hand.

Ashley sits me down and grabs my upper arm, digging her chewed nails into my skin slightly as if to recharge my body with blood.

"What happened?"

"I woke with that chunky hunk-of-dust feeling again, like there was a lump of dry fuzz in my throat. I coughed..."

I began my story, remembering how I knew the gritty sensation was an omen. From years of past experience I'd learned that for me waking with a chalky gullet is synonymous with trouble, a surefire prediction that the near future would hold something terrible.

"When I went to get a glass of water, I saw my Mom scrawling my name on top of a sheet of blank typing paper right beside Toni's. There was a number beside each of our names..."

Toni – 0   Jenna – 0

And it was exactly how I felt.

Mom paused to pour cream in her coffee, stirring. Then scoop, sift, sprinkle, sugar.

Clinkle, clinkle clink, clink.

Her circling spoon sounded musical in the mug, like those tiny chimes you see outside people's doors. I swallowed. Vinegar. Acid down the hatch. Jenna–Zero. I was wondering what I was ever going to do to be more than that.

"Chores," Mom said. "You earn points by doing chores." She called Toni out to the kitchen so she could explain to both of us specifically what she had in mind.

Offering us each a typed copy of a contract and a pen, she told us to sign. It read:

As per the new Point System, I, the undersigned, will complete all tasks on this cleaning list thoroughly and then have them passed by an inspection.

There was a reward at the end of it all, of course. According to the new point system, it was explained to me and Toni, the ten points we earned today would award us the common convenience of not being grounded.

I searched every cranny of the five page typed cleaning list for some captivating clue, some trick door, some alert button that would render this specific system null and void. I would go back to bed and this fluke of having to mathematically earn my basic freedom would never have happened. I'd fall asleep and dream of searching the rainy streets for a message in a bottle. The container would float up from a nearby storm drain, landing at my feet yielding a crisp scroll of paper that would say *help is here now.*

I indulged in the fantasy for minutes on end, exercising the outer reaches of my imagination until something snapped me back to attention. It seems my mouth had been hanging open. Mrs. Root would say little Jenna hadn't changed a bit. Casting my mind back that far made me wonder where everything went wrong.

While Toni was apprehensively signing her copy of the contract, I was already shambling barefoot over the cold basement tile floor to get a jump on the week's laundry. After all, it was going to be a long Saturday. I stayed dressed in my night clothes all morning, suitably clad to get dirty doing the duties on the list, pulling weeds along the fence, cleaning out the closets and cupboards, then all the regular stuff, dusting, mopping, folding towels and sheets, shaking out rugs.

I charged up the vacuum cleaner just as the clock struck noon, rolling it to and fro, kicking up more dust than it was sucking up, tiny particles clouding up the midday sunlight beams coming in the picture window. It was beautiful. It meant I was done cleaning. It meant I was not Zero.

With the hum of the vacuum powered off, I could hear my hunger roaring like a lion in my stomach. Toni was already taking the last forkfuls of cold spaghetti leftovers from a pot in the fridge. When I opened the refrigerator to find my own food, it breathed a frosty mist on my skin. Its contents looked white and insubstantial; milk, butter, bread on chilled shelves.

"Hey Jenna."

My Mom was calling from behind me. Before I turned to answer her, my eyebrow twitched. Another omen. Somehow I knew that Mom's blue eyes would be piercing. And they were. She was almost enraged. The number 'zero' hung over my head, haunting me. My hands wrung together mechanically, turning from a raw splotchy red to a pale green, like that color strip on the litmus test.

"You forgot to sign the contract on the front of this cleaning list," she said.

Ashley puckers her lips to make a silent whistle when I get to this part in the story, involuntarily rolling her eyes.

"That's what I did," I say pointing to her face, "I rolled my eyes."

"Minus ten points for rolling your eyes, Jenna! You're grounded," Mom said.

"That's not fair. You can't do that!" My sister rebelled against the injustice, for the principal of it.

"Minus ten, Toni, for talking back," Mom said. "You're grounded, too."

But my sister couldn't give up the fight with my Mom this time. And I just stood by in awe, watching Toni defend herself in spite of sure defeat.

"That's what you think!" Toni disputed her punishment.

"Minus twenty, then!"

"Whatever."

George came home right then, and we all paused for a second to watch him take a seat on the couch and begin reading the newspaper. Then we started back up where we left off.

"Don't talk back. You're at minus thirty points now. Do you want to keep going?" Mom shouted.

"Might as well," Toni fumed.

"Ok, minus forty."

And the numbers just kept adding up until my sister achieved minus eighty points, a grand effort in rebellion.

"Where's your sister now?" Ashley asks, probing to find out how it ended.

"I don't know."

"Where are you going to go?"

"I don't know."

"I wish you could stay here, but you know my Dad..."

"I know. I guess I'll have to go back home."

"Do you want me to walk you halfway to your house?"

"Ok."

We step out of her front door and head in the direction of my old elementary school, the landmark that stands halfway between my house and Ashley's.

"Hey Ashley," I say, stopping her when we reach the school. I don't want her to leave me just yet.

"Yeah?"

"You see that trophy?" Peering inside the main entrance doors, I point towards the tallest trophy in the school's display. "As a kid I dreamed of having one just like that."

"For what?"

"I don't know. I've just always liked the idea of having a trophy."

"Oh, Jenna. You're going to be great," Ashley looks at me with a comforting smile, grabbing my upper arm. She's assuming I'm still hoping for the great prize that life has planned for me. She thinks I haven't given up on it yet. "We'll both be great," Ashley adds.

"I know." I say, only halfway believing it. I don't dream about greatness these days. I just want to make it through high school. Ashley takes my hand and raises it in solidarity, fingers laced, palm to palm high in the air.

"See you in school," she says.

Waving then and turning in synch we head back to our homes, walking in opposite directions, balanced but still trembling on the very same narrow path, one single tightrope called life.

19

Boomerang
The Next Day

It's a five dollar cab ride from my high school to Marshall, my old downtown Riverston elementary school. That's about a week's worth of my lunch money. Marshall School's campus looks a bit weedier and a bit more cracked than it did several years ago, but it's still pretty well intact.

School's let out for the day, leaving the deserted grounds scattered with a few splintered pencils and worn erasers. The front double doors are stiff but unlocked.

The silent slate colored hallways look much smaller than I remember them being. I find Mrs. Root's classroom just steps away from the entrance doors. I always thought it was such a long, dreadful walk.

I guess memory sometimes slings a boomerang at you, flinging back thoughts that were based not so much on factual truth but more like your best guess, your deepest wishes or your worst fears. I was always convinced I knew for sure that my memory was the exact truth. But here I am, back in my past, seeing my memories differently, wondering if every so-called fact of my life might instead be slightly skewed, overwritten with a little fiction.

I find Frank easily. As I've gotten older, it's become clear how some people are impossible to keep track of, while others are comfortably predictable in their habits and the circles they run in. The great thing about the predictable ones is you can go away awhile and still know right where to find them. The dark circles under Frank's eyes are deep; his face is thin. Still, his eyes sparkle with young aliveness when he recognizes me.

"Hey, Jenna!"

Frank invites me to sit with him on a bench outside the school entrance.

"I don't have much time ta talk today," He says hoarsely. "I'm workin'. Plus I'm gettin' too old to sit for long."

"I just wanted to say hello," I say. But Frank doesn't waste a second on pleasantries.

"I'd like to talk to you blunt if you can forgive me. Jenna, I can see why you came to see me today. This is gonna be hard to hear but if ya really listen, it'll save your life."

His statement gives me a flash of a vision. It's me and my Uncle Tom lying side by side, dead in a coffin.

Frank offers a ripped open roll of LifeSavers for me to take one. It's cherry that's on top. My favorite. I suck on the o-shaped candy and reposition myself on the bench so I can get a good look at Frank. My fingers find an armrest to grip tight, bracing myself for what he's about to say.

"I gotta tell ya," Frank says gently, shaking his head. "I can see you've lost more of your strength, Jenna. You've been giving all your energy to the wind all these years, livin' urgent, dramatic, like you in crisis all the time. Ya look tired."

I fold my arms defensively.

"Nothing's wrong with me," I try to say, but my intention never actually finds my vocal chords. My mouth just opens wide, a fish taking in water. What comes out is a throaty breath, air hauling out from between frozen lips.

"Now there's no need to get upset, Jenna. Don't worry. What I'm tellin' you can be construed as good news. It just depends on how you look at it."

"Good news?" I thread by fingers through the slats in the bench.

"Great news even. See, ya don't know this, but you got choices you can make right now that can change what happens to you tomorrow and the next day and the day after that. Your whole future."

"Like what?"

"Like changin' the habits of ya mind. Twisting your focus from what you don't want to what ya do want. It's that simple."

"But I don't..."

"Look, every child needs love and protection, Jenna. I'm not denyin' that. But the fact is you aren't getting what you need. I know your heart's starved. All I'm sayin' is that can be fixed. All ya gotta do is focus on what feeds it. You know, console yourself."

"But why should I have to..."

"Because it's your *life*. Nobody else is gonna do it for ya, Jenna. Now you don't have time to waste. Remember. God gave you a destiny in this world. But you won't ever reach it if you neglect to first find happiness and satisfaction in your own right. You're old enough now. It's time ta take full charge of ya life. Set your sights on nothing but all the good you can see and dream."

Before I know it, Frank's closing the door to my cab, leaning in my window to add one last thing before I go.

"And Jenna, promise me this, someday when ya choose a man to love for life, let him be calm inside, soft hearted, caring and genuine as you. Make him prove he's the real deal–brave and thankful and willing to stick by your side through it all. You can't afford to accept any less."

"Forty-ninth and Crescent please," I call out a cross street that's near a great patch of forest and farmland, within walking distance from my house. I wave Frank goodbye, roll up the window and relax back into the seat, feeling struck with great warmth and ease as the cab starts moving down toward the train tracks that border my district.

I stare so far past the pedestrians we pass that they completely disappear, creating an empty space in my line of vision to spawn a clear image of what a life and a love like Frank described is going to be like. "You can't afford to accept any less," Frank said.

The taxi gains speed, making the convenience stores and power lines and row homes of downtown Riverston appear to whiz by me.

I've always loved the sensation of speedy departure. I sit still with my hands folded behind my head, looking at the back of the driver's, wondering what he's thinking right now, what his life is all about. Everybody's got a story to tell, that's what I believe.

My taxi tools past browned remnants of earthy summer gardens, making me feel far away from the industrial trains that rumble and roll past my house just two miles from here. The only vibration I can feel now is the hum in my jaw from the revolution of taxi tires.

Taking a glimpse up toward the stormy looking sky I see a thick layer of black clouds begin to block the orange hue of tonight's late autumn sky. The cab shifts to a stop at the end of the sidewalk on Crescent Street.

A low fog has formed the likenesses of two phantoms that appear to be walking in the harvested cornfield ahead of me, making me shiver. I find the courage to follow them toward the mysterious unknown dimming cropland.

What magnifies the eeriness of the phantom dusk is the thump of a rigid praying mantis landing on my coat sleeve. I almost scream but instead go silent, lifting my arm to take a closer look at the bug's profile against the scarlet sky.

My instinctual cringe forks into full curiosity as my eyes adjust to the dark, making out vivid details of its triangular face. The bug looks almost human in its beseeching stillness, turning its head ever so slightly to look directly at me.

I watch closely as the bug leans toward my face with all its mechanical weight. I feel like it's trying to tell me something. Lifting up its front legs in prayer position, the bug leans in toward my face until I get scared enough to scream and flap my arms. The mantis falls away to the ground, but I still feel the need to flee from it, *crunch, crunch, crunch* across the compressed cornfield.

When I shake off the fear and repulsion, I burst into a seizure of giggles with the realization of where I am, breathy heh-heh-heh-heh's coming out hard. How funny I must've looked running from a bug in the middle of a cornfield. I shake and shed tears with almost uncontrollable laughter now.

"Hahahahahahaha," I bleat, bending toward the ground, weakened by the humor I now see in my life in general.

I'm running from my own life, but it doesn't mean I need to. It's *my* life, Frank. Nobody else is going to take charge of it. It's my choice. I can have all the good I can see and dream.

"It'll save your life," Frank said.

I wear those words like a bright yellow lifejacket, cinching them tight around my body's core, leaving me secure enough to keep laughing freely. I shake my head and smile up at the clearing twilight sky.

How does Frank always make everything I need seem so clear? Three stars glimmer through the clouds. I'd better get going. I still have miles to walk before I'm home.

20

What You Focus on Grows
Four Months Later

Because Toni's talking back initiated the great collapse of the Point System, my sister got kicked out of the house in the middle of her twelfth grade school year. She went to live two towns away with my Dad who's always stayed in touch, but who had stopped arranging regular visits like he did just after the divorce. Dad couldn't take me in because he only had one extra bedroom, and anyway, his live in girlfriend happened to be another self professed kid hater.

This past weekend was the first time in a long time I've gone to stay with my Dad. I was curious to see what life was like for Toni sharing an apartment with him and his finicky girlfriend. Ringing the doorbell, I'd hoped they might all greet me at the door like their fourth wheel had finally arrived. Instead I sat on my suitcase and watched Mom drive off, trusting that somebody would soon come to receive me as scheduled. Ringing the bell a second and third time, I eyed the pizza place next door, counting my change to see if I could buy a soda while I waited.

Just as I closed the velcro of my nylon wallet, footsteps galloped in my direction. When the door opened I found it strange to see my father standing inside what looked like a real home again, with a family. I liked the sight of it. I wished I were part of it.

Dad's entryway exhibited an artful red color, giving a classic look to the place, offering a hint of old world elegance typical of the properties along the streets around the nearby college.

Toni dragged my borrowed suitcase up Dad's ample stairs. I took in the decor on the way up, shocked by how different it was from the handful of bachelor pads Dad's had during the seven or eight years he'd been living on his own. The white plaster walls made the place seem spacious and European. Vast warm colored rooms were filled with plush furniture and collector teddy bears, the lively décor a strong contrast to the barren suburban interiors I've spied through the windows in my own neighborhood.

From the privacy of her bedroom, Toni divulged all the details of her comings and goings with a group of artsy people she met at her new high school, handing me photographic proof that they existed, that they actually do all hang out together all night long, exactly like the cute, fiery, and lively graduates in *St. Elmo's Fire*. I could see a green tint of envy reflecting off of the glossy photo surfaces. Because she now had everything she'd always wanted. Everything I'd always wanted.

Visiting her only reminded me of how crowded and limiting my own indoor space at home has become. It's seemed to slowly shrink down to the size of those miniature dollhouses with tiny rooms that you can hardly get your hands into. Maybe it's just that the world feels a lot smaller to me in general now that it's winter again.

It's this time of year when the sound of metal and machines ricochets through the naked trees and spindly thicket behind my house, rattling my window pane enough to itch my inner ears. With no leaves on the trees, there's not even a buffer of green to block the rambling railroad yards and stop the sound of the car engines that roar down the main street adjacent to the tracks.

I often look out my bedroom window just to frown at the noise, feeling the need to show the world my disapproval for its deafening bleakness. And then I remember to shift my thoughts, console myself.

While tucked tightly into my heavy warm blankets, I make a practice of imagining my perfect future in great detail, jotting down in my journal any thoughts that come to mind. Each night I easily fill dozens of pages with scrawled yearnings, my pencil pulling at an invisible strand of feeling from my insides, craving to be unraveled.

Writing with great passion, I spend hundreds of winter evening hours loosening the knots inside my psyche, focusing only on what I want my life to look like, like Frank said to. Every night I stay up to write as much as I can before my body feels absolutely forced to lie down, yielding to gravity and sweet sleep.

One night while asleep, I dream something different about Grandma. She's looking pregnant as a pumpkin, her belly unnaturally protruding from her dress.

"It's a tumor," the doctors will later say in real life. "The size of a grapefruit on her ovary." That means Grandma will need a caregiver, her daughter, my Mom, to give her the right pills on the right days, to buy her special cushions and pillows and a walker.

As the days fall close to Christmas, Grandma tumbles out of her bed more and more often, jarring me awake.

"Jennnaaaaaa," she calls.

Being the closest to her room, I spring out of bed and run through the dark, wondering what condition I will find her in this time. She's fallen again, her poor frail body silhouetted against her light pink nightie, which is soaked with spilled urine from the bedside toilet. I toss a folded towel on the puddle. Grandma's blue eyes flash up towards me with unspoken surrender.

My Grandma feels so small and frail in my hands. Her bony arm is hardly a help holding onto. So I bend down to grab her by the waist.

"Arms up over your head now," I say when I get her standing. It's what my Nanna said to get my shirt changed when I was a child. Grandma's wet nightgown easily slips off.

"Hold on to the toilet rails for a minute," I tell her while propping up the fallen basin, returning it upright and stable next to her. "I'll be right back."

A warm washcloth can stay warm all the way down the hall from the bathroom if it's tightly cupped in your hands. Soapy cloth on wrinkled skin, I really see how delicate her aging body is. It doesn't seem fair that there's a mound of tissue in her tummy too, growing, devouring her body. I tuck Grandma back into bed clean but naked, smoothing her soft silver hair that's shimmering like thin filaments against her faded yellow pillowcase.

Mom and I have been searching for a nursing home for Grandma, one that's better than all the others. It's tough finding one without the strange sight of IV tubes rolling next to walking patients or the smell of sickness hitting you the second you walk inside. As we tour facility after facility,

I try to stay focused on whatever good I can find, even though I sense that patients are tired of pressing nurse call buttons in vain for water, more painkillers, a nurse, an answer, any answer. I think of my notebook and my dreams for a better future as I watch nurses raise metal bars around each bed–perhaps a subliminal suggestion that illness belongs in a cage. I don't want to go to any more nursing homes. But I will. Almost every day. Because we've found one to move Grandma to, the absolute best one we can afford.

Things get worse before they get better, right? I think of my notebook. I keep writing, keep dreaming. I believe that I am on my way to something better.

Throughout the blustery winter I get stirred awake by what sounds like a boom in the middle of the night, like Grandma has fallen again.

"Jennnaaaaaa…" I hear her voice, too, and that sends a chill right through me because I know she's not home anymore. She's in a bed across the city.

I wish we could stop visiting her. But Grandma needs us. We have to keep going there.

Jenna, keep going.

"How's that?" Mom asks her dying mother after rearranging her pillows. It's been months and still the nurses have been leaving Grandma with a thick stack of pillows stuffed behind her thinning head, making her chin almost touch her chest.

"Here let me lift you so you can sit up for our visit."

Mom dotes on Grandma, instinctively easing the pain of her bed sores by doubling up the foam mattress under her legs. Washing Grandma's hair however, will take some help. Mom's arranged for Toni to come help hold Grandma's scalp while Mom shampoos and combs what short white hair Grandma has left so it lays clean and soft, flat and attractive.

"Hey, Jenna!" Toni walks in Grandma's room with open arms for a sister to sister hug, her green button down cardigan sweater fanning out from her long black skirt. She looks so different to me, but I can't place what's new about her. Her braces are still on. Maybe it's that her short haircut is growing out, giving her a more soft, feminine look. She actually looks happy to see me, or just happy in general.

"Toni!" I squeal at the joy of finally having someone there to laugh with me, old army buddies. We immediately start giggling I guess the only way we know to ease the tension, to find relief from the ongoing reminder of the ruthlessness of cancer.

And as we carry on with sisterly giddiness over the remainder of the visit, Mom and Grandma join in on the laughing, too, until wouldn't you know it, all of a sudden all of the heaviness from the room drops off like lead.

With that heaviness gone and amusement in its place, the sensation we all feel is perhaps best described as a temporary state of being cured. It seems to me, at least for this moment in time, that our joyful commotion carries just enough optimism to remedy Grandma's disease.

And what's more, I sense that the heightened charm in this room also has the potential to dispense a much larger antidote—the cheerful and spontaneous reversal of every single ailment, every last complaint or misfortune or tribulation that would so much as dare to come near us ever again.

• • •

It's the very first spring-like day of the year. Bulbs are already in bloom, filling the air with sweet scents and joyful color.

At last, life is teeming in the world outside.

Alas, life is fading from inside Grandma's body.

When I talk to Grandma for the last time, she tells me she's been dreaming of her late husband John who died over forty years ago.

"I can't wait to meet him again," she says of the Grandfather I never met. It's the most personal thing I've ever heard her say. I search the whole landscape of her face just then, looking for something familiar. When I come up short, I'm forced to admit that I never really understood who she was to me. It's hard to look at her in such a weakened state and believe that I could have been angry at her all these years, but the truth is I have been. I've hated that she lived her life as fragile, vulnerable and guarded as she did.

How can you live a life so guarded in fear like that?

I would never live my life that way.

Except I've already started to.

And I want to blame somebody for it.

But you can't really blame anyone for anything once you've grown up.

There's a point where just have to get yourself where you need to be. I didn't forget what Frank told me about consoling myself. So today I'll find my comfort in total honesty, admitting to all the pity and the guilt and the anger I felt all these years.

And then I'll let it go.

"Goodbye Grandma."

When I walk out of Grandma's nursing home for the last time, I stretch my arms toward the sky and take a good long minute to pause and deliberately appreciate the emergence, the vibrancy, the intention of the tulip bulbs that beam yellow and red all around me under the springtime sun.

Grandma might have passed, but I'm still alive, and I plan on letting the world know about it.

21

Chemistry
Age 16, January 1988

From deep emotions, the sensual power of the elements, and the poetic explorations of the mind there emerges an impassioned curiosity that elicits physical chemistry. This romantic allure between boy and girl is often mistaken for a boiling point of attraction–the kind that makes your hair stand up on your arms and your blood rush around, looking for where the thrill is.

But what appeals to me more is a fever of the heart– a great magnetism in the presence of something enduring. Love. In a perceptive girl's world, it's easy to tell whether a boy's objective has to do with devotion. And when it doesn't, it only feels right to move on and keep the door open for more genuine intentions.

Senior year Chemistry class, for me, has nothing to do with the Periodic Table of the Elements that hangs over our heads, flat and colorless, full of numbers and symbols and squares. It has to do with a sentimental chemistry that's already found me, through a boy named Mark who sits one desk to my left.

At the start of class every day this brown-haired artist draws my attention by offering me a giant, thick lipped sideways smile, a syrupy kind of smile that creeps across my senses. Mark's "good morning" is focused and deliberate, spoken respectfully to a maturing young woman who's getting clearer about what's good for her.

In class Mark talks to me like I'm his best friend, leaning over to look at my test scores, congratulating me for a job well done, passing me notes with funny pictures on my bad days. When he asks me, I tell him, "yes" I will go on a date.

He picks me up in a rugged Toyota Corolla that is not so much a car as a shell that you can see through, a paint stripped metal box on wheels. It could be ready to stop dead at any moment but I imagine it as a chariot. If this car is the best we have then it will take us where we need to go.

And it does take us places—settings where we begin to build a history between us. We don't go to movies or malls. We go to the overgrown fields where development is encroaching but hasn't yet plowed. When we're lucky, the smell of the farmland is smoky and thick like a mix of rain and fire. We dance on picnic tables in the parks and we creak on the swings in the playgrounds of our city. Clustering together on curbs in the suburbs we keep warm watching skateboarders wheel over wet leaves.

With clinging arms around bony waists, we talk and we walk and we laugh. Speeding off into the great wide open, I wind down all the car windows, letting winter air roar through our hair, making a mess of us. Mark parks the car on the side of a rural road to share his personal hiding place, his bridge over troubled water in the woods, knowing he can trust me with such a secret. And when he does, a cool drizzle drums the canopy above our heads.

Mark's openness of heart shows me he can handle the closeness it takes to build something lasting. As winter turns to spring, I exercise new levels of openness because I sense he's staying present. This intimacy gets mixed with defensiveness when my feelings for him deepen. He can really hurt me if he wants to. That gives me new doubts about this whole thing.

"I love you, Jenna."

Mark bravely asserts his heartfelt affection one temperate evening in the middle of a patch of new green grass. I know he's telling the truth. But there's another truth that trumps love. It's fear. Mine is that one of us eventually has to be hurt. That's just how relationships work.

I remember it from the innocent years, the days when I was just starting to learn that life and love ultimately turn into a war where everything gets damaged beyond repair. And when everything gets broken that badly, you can't ever fix it. You can never, ever make it all new again. So even though this has a chance of being good and lasting and healthy, over the coming months I will take an imaginary chisel and blow by blow, intentionally hammer cracks into the stable foundation that Mark and I have built.

Mark in Art Class, Senior Year

22

White for Innocence
Age 17, June 1989

About seven hundred pairs of feet are rumbling over the wooden bleachers in my high school gymnasium. Students and parents keep stamping up and across the risers, only to sit down, scoot over, and shuffle some more on its surface.

The massive wood structure rattles and rocks. People chat and wave. Girls cinch down their short skirts so the three hundred people on the bleachers across the gym can't see their underwear. This movement helps pacify my nervous butterflies. The vibration makes me less dizzy, my palms less sweaty. But I'm still thirsty.

I'm donning a white cap and gown, red lipstick and a black tassel–Riverston High School colors. Tonight's the last night I'm singing with this choir. Forty-five round mouths are about to synchronize and harmonize in joy for the rite of passage that is called graduation. There are black and white gowns on stage with black-and white-skinned hands holding black music books in front of red cheeks. The songs we're singing have lyrics about being all you can be. We sing words like "this is your one moment in time" and "never stop believing you can fly." As the words come out, I want to recapture them and tuck them under my skin somewhere for safe keeping.

After the ceremonies end, flash bulbs flicker all around like strobes. Dad snaps photos of Mark next to me in our graduation caps.

Mark and I patched things up as we went along this year. We still had our differences, but he taught me something I didn't ever see coming. He showed me that even though it's true that broken things can't be completely fixed, sometimes something even better happens. When people get creative, they can take the tattered pieces and use them to rebuild something so much more sturdy and beautiful.

As the parents and classmates make their way home from the school grounds, Mark and I linger hand in hand under the ceremony lights and silently watch the programs get swept away. Rotating me towards him, he twirls me out into a dance, sending my long black graduation tassel spinning up and out. It's a moment of innocence like I remember feeling with my sister as a very young kid—the kind of purity where you let your heart lead you to dance all you want in the middle of a public place.

I want to keep on dancing like this.

And so I do.

And Mark.

Dances with me.

Until I'm done.

• • •

In the pink light of dawn, when the very first early morning breeze lifts me awake, I get this knowing feeling that there's nothing in the universe but me and God. And then it's gone. And I'm afraid again.

The finality of graduation left me questioning the stability of my future. My whole foundation was built on an accumulation of overwhelming circumstances; parents fighting, nuclear sirens, cyanide poisoning, blindfolded hostages, grandma dying, crisis after crisis, all of it magnified by my deep-thinking mind. I'm afraid I have it all collected inside me, either hidden or denied. And I hate that it'll have to stay there until a later time.

This is the stage of my life I've been waiting for. Having total freedom without limitation. I'm dying to dive into life drastically–to help every suffering creature quickly, frantically. I've lost years where I could have been serving the world with passion and energy. But I got ensnared in a long, onerous struggle that left no room for recovery.

An afflicted warrior still looking for someone to save, I want to tell whoever is listening that help is on its way. Is my childhood dream still possible, to do good for the world, even if I haven't yet recovered, even if my own help never came?

"You can't afford to accept any less."

This is the final thing Frank said to me when I saw him last. He was talking about love when he said it. But I think he was also talking about life–suggesting that I could start by helping one single suffering creature, myself, by accepting only what's best for me.

I take a moment to envision myself plucking good experiences like flowers that swing in the wind with wildness, provisions, and beauty. Just imagining it makes my muscles relax, my diaphragm slacken. I could have that easy kind of life if I'd just stop feeling guilty and let myself tend to the longing child who waits inside me.

There's serenity here at the edge of such an important decision. The sunrise is low and red, a glowing heart on the horizon. I watch it float higher, brightening the rooftops of my neighborhood. Soon the dawn will become full daylight.

23

The Light
The Week After Graduation

I had another premonition the day Mark took me to visit our old favorite high school meeting spots. We were so twisted together on that day, like two sticky, rubbery people, falling out of the car, wild and loose. We felt free together, bolting up and down the marble steps outside my church's massive wooden doors. We gave chase, laughed and wrestled together in the grass underneath the climbing tree, the one where I first called "help" to Frank about eight years back.

I giggled hard when Mark playfully pinned me to the ground, pushing in vain against a grip that was too strong to break free from. I teasingly threatened that if he didn't let go, I'd make him listen to me tell my story again about how I met Frank.

"There was a man chasing me and Toni through the streets of this neighborhood," I began.

Mark smiled and softened, flopping down on the grass beside me. "You can tell me all you want about Frank," Mark said. "I think he's a great man. Actually, if you think about it, he's probably the reason we're still together."

I yawned with sudden sleepiness.

"And so then Frank came out of nowhere to help me when I yelled *fire*," I continued.

"I know." Mark pulled me in close to his body until we were nestled tightly together under the shade of the climbing tree.

Before long, I'd drifted to sleep and had begun dreaming in vivid detail. The dream began with a sudden breeze that was circling around the church. The wind was so blustery that it caused a vibrant yellow colored leaflet to ripple against the church door. It was flapping fast, demanding attention. In the dream I got up from underneath the tree to see what the flyer said.

It was a funeral notice. With Frank's picture on it. Those kind eyes were beaming at me as friendly as the first day he said "I unna-stan."

Frank *did* understand.

Like nobody else in the world.

The dream continued. I knelt on the ground in front of the church, wondering why I never asked Frank how to say goodbye to someone after they've already left. The great breaking inside me felt so real. It was like all the pain I'd ever felt in my life, all at once.

The dream changed scenes just then to a crowd that was funneling into a pitch dark church for Frank's funeral. Each mourner was lighting a small candle on their way in until the church was glowing with three hundred tiny orange flames. As one of the memorial service attendees I could hear every word that was spoken by the pastor with remarkable clarity.

"When life turns the lights out on you, you're never, ever in the dark," the minister addressed the congregation using a small silver handheld microphone "because the light of truth always has a way of shining in earnest." His words caused the church to buzz with drones and murmurs, hundreds of hmmms and hissing whispered yesssss's. Spreading his left arm out to demonstrate the brilliance of the candlelight he continued on.

"Our friend Frank knew something about shining his light, even though he didn't have much but darkness in his early life. I think his favorite saying was, 'You won't have no future until you shine a spotlight on your past.' Frank gave us an example of how to take your past and let it make you richer.

Frank didn't cling to his past or dwell on it. He didn't try to deny it or bury it away either. He just dredged it all up and moved it out, using the pain of the process to press on and grow. I've known him a long time, watching him as he grew, and I've seen him truly refine himself, using every opportunity he could to keep his heart's integrity. His example reminded me personally to be humble, to put my own pain out in the light, and say, 'This is what happened. And these are my feelings about it.'

"Now Frank wasn't perfect, that's for sure. I'm certain you've all got your stories about how his straightforward manner could get under your skin." The pastor paused to let three hundred people laugh heartily. I could feel the warmth in the church growing. We all shuffled, stirred and relaxed again.

"Yeah, he was pretty blunt with just exactly what you didn't want to hear. Maybe some would say he was even a bit reckless. But the thing is he always told the truth–from his heart. In fact, by his late age I'd say he pretty nearly mastered love. After all, he gave it away freely. He delivered grace to so many of us at this service today just by listening with his time and attention. What a great gift he was." The crowd nodded and talked softly for a moment.

"Being true to his reputation," the pastor sighed, "Frank was thinking of us when he died. He asked that his funeral be filled with candles that represent the light in each and every one of us.

So I will close this eulogy with a poem called *I Light a Flame* he'd always kept in his wallet. Frank's grandfather wrote it for him when he was a young man. Frank credits this poem for changing the entire course of his life.

It goes like this:

I light a flame for you
and for your perfect imperfection;
for your blind, unkind mistakes
and their courageous redirection.
Light glows as you shed your status
for the sake of being true.
Light flows to warm the liar living
in the frightened part of you.
Walk on. You're glowing bright
as you embrace your brilliant weakness.
I pray you treat yourself with
kindness, patience and forgiveness.
Remember there will be days and nights
where darkness comes to find you.
But you're always full of a certain light.
Let the candle's wick remind you.

That's where the dream ended. Mark leaned on his elbow beside me, paying tender attention to me sleeping. Searching Mark's face helped anchor me awake.

"Wow, you were dreaming," he said.

"Ready to go?" I ignored his words, gathering myself up hastily. I was loath to mention the dream, the premonition, afraid to face the fact that Frank didn't have much time left to live.

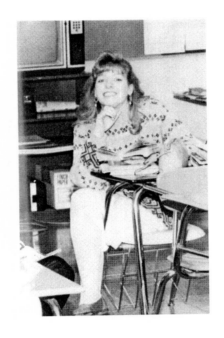

A photo from our high school yearbook, 1989

24

Victory
August, 1989

When my car makes impact it sounds like a bomb.

My attention was on the birds on the expressway who hesitate to fly away when cars rush toward them. *Why do some birds risk clinging to the road,* I wondered, *while others flock upwards staying safely in flight until all danger passes?*

All the pictures of my life are flicking through my mind like a playing card slideshow. The last card casts an image of me on my eighteenth birthday. We lost Uncle Tom when he was eighteen. I'd always been determined to live long past that age. I hadn't expected this accident.

There should be pain here inside these two thousand pounds of twisted metal. Blood ought to be sprinkled on the shattered glass, this crushed roof. But there's nothing but the smell of bread from a nearby bakery. It gives a buttery warmth to the air over the expressway.

Moving cars stream with purpose and direction on the road outside this fractured windshield. They're flowing like energy through my anatomy. Billions of tiny particles split and dance, losing all material form, specs of life blending together. There is a raw silence which becomes a symphony. It delivers lightness of body. The events of recent months feather through my jostled consciousness.

After graduation I had moved into Mark's apartment where we battled regularly, passionately, like my parents did. Like I vowed I never would. I lived there out of love, but also out of urgency. Mom had become progressively more volatile and unpredictable, suffering terrible emotional swings. George had fully evaporated into passive capitulation. Toni lived out of town at her college but still called Dad's house her permanent home, while Dad stayed characteristically unworried, voluntarily unaware of the conditions, factors and context of my circumstances. My family, once merely broken, had now splintered off considerably and it settled that way.

My first steps outside my home were a stumbling mix of absurd resourcefulness and habitual desperation. During the summer months, I reported to a tense office with a touchy-feely boss because I needed the money. On my nights off I searched for a second job, filling out applications at malls and restaurants, knowing I couldn't fit into those tiny boxes on generic employment applications.

In meager weeks I'd search for stray change and exchange it at the bank just for the feel of having paper bills. Mark borrowed a few dollars from friends here and there to buy damaged cans of soup from the grocery store where he worked. Our four roommates shared the rent.

If it wasn't for the Exxon Valdez oil spill, my passion for service to the world might have lost my attention. Watching 11 million gallons of oil turning seabirds black in Alaska reminded me to adhere to my mission with unbending dedication. I wanted to do good things for the world and so I would. I had already been accepted to study science at a distant university in the fall. It would buy me some time to discover the things about myself I never had the space or energy to look for at home.

I didn't know how I would pay for the education, but there had always been obstacles in my way, and I'd made it this far.

Screaming sirens blast. With a shaky arm I silence the thundering static on the car radio and hug my arms across my chest, feeling chilled. Leaning sideways causes the door to unhinge like a broken wing. A lapful of windshield glass spills to the asphalt. Stepping out, I crush scattered shards into fine white powder feeling inexplicably pardoned from any physical ramification.

The traffic's back and forth movement speaks to me. Streams of drivers dodge strewn pieces of plastic, glass and metal from the accident's excessive wreckage. This spot of highway has temporarily become a short stretch of scattered impediments, an obstacle course of dangers, stealing drivers' ease of uninhibited flow. They're speeding into unexpected hurdles on their way to where they want to go. Some of them will swerve and lose control while others will react in time to avoid any obstruction to their destination. Each circumstance has the potential to redirect the passengers entirely, inviting curious travelers down an easy, airy path that promises deliverance to that place called Victory.

• • •

Mark and I wander out under the stars in the humid August night air to watch the forecasted lunar eclipse. With eyes on the sky, our smallish earthly bodies bask on the warm sidewalk outside our apartment. The blackness of the sky looks bold, alive. White pins of starlight appear to twirl in circles as they sparkle.

"Frank doesn't exactly exist," I confess to Mark without taking my eyes off the sky.

Mark's response to my admission tells me he understood the truth about Frank all along–much more than I'd have realized. Frank, as a person, was all too unreal to totally believe I guess. But Frank, as an idea, was exactly what life had planned to guide me through the trenches of the heart. Mark knew that Frank's voice, my consciousness, helped me–that it will always help me.

I still had a lot more to learn about the source of that inner voice but that would have to wait. There was some maturing I would need to do first. My only focus for now was on finding my way to tomorrow.

"You ever look at the sky and try to count the billions of stars?" I ask Mark, returning my curiosity to the heavens.

Mark squeezes the softly curled ends of my hair, tugging ever so lightly to make me feel it's going to be alright.

"Uncountable," he says.

I glance over at my boyfriend, amazed by his perception and patience. Through my tears, I can see the full moon in his eyes.

"What if the sky was nothing but a mirror? What if everyone we know is just a star in the sky lighting up the earth–just points of light from a distance, all shining, all meant to be?"

"We are, Jenna. Never doubt it," Mark whispers sincerely.

The face made of shadowy craters in the full moon becomes recognizable to me for the first time. An arc of darkness sweeps its cheek with slow grace. The eclipse has begun.

My Mom once said the darkness and clouds would always pass by eventually.

"Soon the sunshine will come find us," she said.

I remember.

It was exactly what I needed to hear back then.

And though I always wanted to believe it, I never knew for sure.

Until now.

Nanna's House 1974

Jenna 1973

Jenna today

There's more online at www.jennaforrest.com.

CPSIA information can be obtained at www.ICGtesting.com
Printed in the USA
LVOW12s2103211014

409817LV00001B/117/P